Brexit

by Nicholas Wallwork

Brexit For Dummies®

Published by: **John Wiley & Sons, Inc.,** 111 River Street, Hoboken, NJ 07030-5774, www.wiley.com

Copyright © 2019 by John Wiley & Sons, Inc., Hoboken, New Jersey

Published simultaneously in Canada

For general information on our other products and services, please contact our Customer Care Department within the U.S. at 877-762-2974, outside the U.S. at 317-572-3993, or fax 317-572-4002. For technical support, please visit https://hub.wiley.com/community/support/dummies.

Wiley publishes in a variety of print and electronic formats and by print-on-demand. Some material included with standard print versions of this book may not be included in e-books or in print-on-demand. If this book refers to media such as a CD or DVD that is not included in the version you purchased, you may download this material at http://booksupport.wiley.com. For more information about Wiley products, visit www.wiley.com.

ISBN 978-1-119-60122-7 (pbk); ISBN 978-1-119-60125-8 (ebk); ISBN 978-1-119-60126-5 (ebk)

Manufactured in the United States of America

C10010793_060419

Contents at a Glance

Table of Contents

Introduction

Welcome to *Brexit For Dummies* and thank you for choosing me to guide you through the tricky topic of Brexit.

When the United Kingdom (UK) voted to leave the European Union (EU) on June 23, 2016, the result sent shockwaves around the world. In the years since, we've witnessed a complex (and seemingly never-ending) negotiation process, all sorts of political point-scoring, and a whole heap of steaming uncertainty. This book is designed to cut through all that and get to the critical information you need to understand and navigate Brexit.

Let me say upfront that I'm not a politician, I'm not a political journalist, I'm not an economist, and I'm not a civil servant. So, what, you might be wondering, qualifies me to write *Brexit For Dummies?*

I'm a British business owner, investor, and entrepreneur. I own and run several businesses in the UK, each one impacted by Brexit in slightly different ways. This gives me a solid foundation to write a book aimed at others — especially those in business in the UK — who have been scratching their heads at the news and wondering what Brexit means for them.

And what if you're not in the UK? What if you're in Europe or the United States, for instance, and you find yourself looking at Brexit from the outside in, wondering what the heck is going on? If that's the case, I welcome you to our (not very) sunny shores and look forward to giving you a Briton's perspective on Brexit.

About This Book

Few words have the power to divide the nation like *Brexit.* Walk into any pub, shop, or office in the UK and ask the people inside what they think about Brexit, and you'll get very different answers. In fact, the Brexit referendum divided opinion like nothing I've ever seen before. People who grew up together voted in opposite directions. Meals among friends descended into heated political debate. The "B-word" was banned from many a family gathering.

Few Brits were or are "on the fence" about Brexit. In my experience, most people in the UK feel pretty strongly one way or the other. In addition, most newspapers skewed heavily for or against Brexit.

Because of this, unbiased information about Brexit can be hard to come by. Yet, regardless of which way we voted, neutral information is exactly what we all need at this point in the Brexit journey. The UK has voted to leave the EU; when it does leave, we must all begin to navigate the UK's new relationship with the EU.

For example, what happens to EU citizens living in the UK (and vice versa)? What might change for British businesses that export/import goods to/from the EU? How should businesses prepare for what comes next? What positive opportunities lie ahead for companies in the post-Brexit world?

In these pages, I answer all these questions and more — and always in an impartial way. You might say I'm on the fence and I'm staying there, at least for the duration of this book! Come join me up here. There's plenty of room, and the view's great.

Precisely because I'm a political "outsider," I can deliver the unbiased information you need. In other words, I'm not trying to get you to vote for me, and I'm not trying to "spin" the facts to further my own agenda. Like you, I'm just trying to deal with Brexit, strip away the hype, and prepare myself and my businesses for life after Brexit.

So, as you may have guessed, impartiality is a core concept of this book. Here are two other concepts that *Brexit For Dummies* is built upon:

>> We get it — Brexit is a serious topic, with serious, real-world implications. But do we have to be bored to tears (or, worse, whipped up into a furious rage) while reading about it? I don't think so. That's why this book is designed to explore Brexit in an interesting, engaging way, as well as in a balanced way.

>> The UK's relationship with the EU is complex and wide-reaching. To cover every aspect of negotiations and the UK's future relationship with the EU would be impossible in a short, easy-to-read guide like this. That's why this book leans more toward the business aspects of Brexit, as opposed to implications for areas like security, defense, foreign policy, and so on. For many people, whether they own a business or are employed in a business, it's the business implications that present (potentially) the biggest headaches.

One final, practical thing to note about this book: Within this book, you may note that some web addresses break across two lines of text. If you're reading this book in print and want to visit one of these web pages, simply key in the web address exactly as it's noted in the text, pretending as though the line break doesn't exist. If you're reading this as an e-book, you've got it easy — just click the web address to be taken directly to the web page.

Foolish Assumptions

Most authors have a specific audience in mind as they write. I'm no different. So, while I was writing this book, I made some assumptions about you as a reader:

» You're looking for a balanced guide to Brexit, written by someone who's not out to score political points or put the fear of God into you. You want the facts, and you want to be left to your own political opinions, thanks very much.

» You sometimes feel like you're suffering from information overload or Brexit exhaustion. You know you *need* to be informed about Brexit; you just want someone to pull together the "must-know" info in one easy-to-read resource.

» You run a business or work in a business, and you're concerned how Brexit might impact your everyday business processes. You want to know how to assess the potential impact and make a realistic plan for the future.

If that sounds like you (and I hope it does!), this book is just what you need.

Icons Used in This Book

To help you get the most out of this book, I highlight key points of advice with the following eye-catching icons. Look out for these helpful symbols throughout the book and you can be sure you're picking up on the most important info:

REMEMBER

You'll no doubt want to commit certain info from this book to memory. But how do you know what's key and what's not? Check out this icon for the must-read Brexit info that you'll want to remember.

TIP

I use this icon to highlight handy hints and tips that are designed to save you time or effort, or generally make your life a little bit easier as you navigate the world of Brexit.

WARNING

This icon draws your eye to things to avoid, or areas where professional advice is a must.

TECHNICAL STUFF

Anything marked with the Technical Stuff icon is, well, a bit technical. It's not essential to your understanding of the subject at hand, but if you're a wonky sort, you'll probably find this material fascinating!

Beyond This Book

In addition to the book you have in your hand, you can access some helpful extra content online. Check out the free Cheat Sheet for bonus Brexit content. You can access it by going to www.dummies.com and entering **Brexit For Dummies** in the Search box.

You can also find lots of additional information for business owners at www.dummies.com. Whether you're just starting a business or looking to expand your skills in networking, leadership, project management or whatever, you'll find plenty of inspiration and advice on the website.

Where to Go from Here

Right then, where do you want to start?

One of the great things about *For Dummies* books is that they're designed to be read in any way that works for you. So, if you want to read the entire book from cover to cover, go for it.

But maybe you have a burning desire to understand how the UK came to hold a referendum on EU membership. In which case, skip ahead to Chapter 2 and read about the UK's rocky relationship with the EU. Need to know how Brexit affects employees from the EU? Chapter 7 is what you're looking for. Interested in potential business opportunities after Brexit? Turn to Chapter 11, my friend. You can pick and choose the chapters that appeal to you most, so flip through the table of contents and take it from there.

Not sure where to begin? That's fine, too. Just turn the page and see what comes next.

1

Getting Familiar with Brexit

Chapter **1**

What Is Brexit and What Does It Mean for You?

n 2016, the United Kingdom (UK), which comprises Great Britain and Northern Ireland, voted to leave the European Union (EU).

Europe had become a bitterly divisive issue in the country, and especially within the ruling Conservative Party. The country was essentially split down the middle, with "Remainers" on one side, arguing that the UK benefited greatly from membership in the EU, and "Leavers" ("Brexiters" or the even more jaunty-sounding "Brexiteers") on the other, arguing that it was time to take back control from the EU.

The prime minister at the time, David Cameron, hoped that a referendum would settle the issue for at least a generation. Firmly on the Remain side, he took a gamble that the voting public would choose to stay in the EU, and the more Eurosceptic elements of his party would have to put up and shut up. But things didn't quite work out the way he planned, and the public voted, albeit by a narrow margin, to say *au revoir*, *adios*, and *auf Wiedersehen* to the EU. And so began the British exit from the EU: Brexit.

In this chapter, I take you on a whistle-stop tour through the referendum, the Brexit process, and what the UK's departure from the EU means for the UK and Europe — not to mention us regular folk who have to navigate this incredibly complex labyrinth.

The Votes Are In, But How Did We Get Here?

The 2016 referendum wasn't the UK's first vote on Europe. In 1975, there was a referendum on whether the UK should stay in the European Economic Community (EEC; see the sidebar "Do you speak Brexit?," later in this chapter, for a breakdown of all the Brexit lingo you need to know). The result of that referendum was a firm "Yes, please, we'd like to stay in," with 67.2 percent of voters voting in favor.

Looking at the 2016 results in more detail

Fast-forward a generation, and the 2016 referendum turned the previous result on its head, but by a narrower margin. Overall, 51.89 percent voted to leave the EU, while 48.11 percent voted to stay in.

But the UK is made up of four different countries, and, interestingly, the individual countries voted in quite different ways:

» England voted Leave, by 53.38 percent to 46.62 percent.

» Scotland voted Remain, by 62 percent to 38 percent.

» Wales voted Leave, by 52.53 percent to 47.47 percent.

» Northern Ireland voted Remain, by 55.78 percent to 44.22 percent.

REMEMBER

Why did people vote to leave? Well, the answer will vary depending on who you ask. But some of the key reasons Leavers wanted out of the EU included the following:

>> Having to make financial contributions to the EU's annual budget

>> Free movement of people and the perception that immigration from Europe was too high

>> Wanting the UK to be able to negotiate its own trade deals, instead of negotiating as part of the EU bloc

>> Perceived lack of UK "sovereignty" or control, with the UK being bound by EU rules and regulations

Meanwhile, those on the Remain side pointed out that, as with any EU member, the UK directly benefited from the EU budget — and from free movement of people and the EU single market, for that matter. Many Remainers also felt that the UK should be integrating closer with Europe, not distancing itself from its closest neighbours and biggest trading partner. Read more about these knotty referendum issues in Chapter 2.

Understanding the UK's complex relationship with Europe

It's fair to say that the UK never really bought into the dream of a fully integrated Europe, and it kept Europe at arm's length whenever possible. When the EEC was formed in 1957, the UK didn't sign up. And when the UK did apply, in the 1960s, its entry was vetoed by a skeptical France.

REMEMBER

The UK eventually joined the club in the 1970s but remained, in its own way, distant from Europe. Over the years, the UK has voted against or opted out of key EU arrangements, such as the euro single currency or the Schengen passport-free travel area (see the nearby sidebar "Do you speak Brexit?").

Throughout the 1990s and later, as Europe moved toward greater integration (political and social integration, as well as economic integration), Euroscepticism really began to grow in the UK. Nationalist parties like the UK Independence Party (UKIP), whose main mission was to get the UK out of the EU, grew in popularity and tapped into voter concerns around immigration in a very effective way. UKIP finally won a seat in the UK Parliament in 2014; a year later, in the run-up to the UK general election, the Conservative Party manifesto included the promise of an EU referendum. The Conservatives won, and the referendum took place a year later.

Read more about the UK's past relationship with Europe in Chapter 2.

DO YOU SPEAK BREXIT?

Brexit is a topic that's dominated by political and economic jargon, and loaded with more acronyms than you can shake a stick at. What does it all mean? Read on.

- **European Union (EU):** The political and economic union that comprises 28 member states, with a total population of around 500 million. That's including the UK, however — there will be 27 member states when the UK leaves the EU. So, when you hear people talk about the EU27, they're referring to the remaining 27 countries of the EU, excluding the UK. The EU is built upon four key principles, or freedoms: free movement of people, goods, services, and money across all member states.

- **Eurozone:** Those members of the EU that have adopted the euro currency. Not all EU members are part of the eurozone; the UK, for example, chose not to adopt the euro, while newer EU members like Bulgaria and Romania are working toward adopting the euro.

- **Schengen Area:** An area of passport- and border-free travel within Europe. It comprises most (not all) EU countries, plus some non-EU countries, such as Switzerland. The UK did not participate in Schengen.

- **European Economic Community (EEC):** In very simple terms, the precursor to the EU. Created in 1957, it aimed to bring about greater economic integration between member countries in Europe. The UK wasn't an original member of the EEC, and it didn't end up joining until the 1970s. When the EU was eventually formed in the 1990s (reflecting the fact that European integration was now about much more than economic cooperation), the EEC was essentially folded into the EU.

- **Single market (or common market):** The EU's free trade area. The single market means participating countries can trade freely with each other without trade barriers (like tariffs). For this to happen, all countries in the EU single market generally follow the same rules, regulations, and standards, and accept the free movement of people, goods, services, and money. You cannot be a member of the single market without accepting free movement of people.

- **EU customs union:** Different from the single market. A customs union means all members agree to charge the same tariffs on imports from outside the union. You can be a member of the customs union (and apply the same agreed-upon tariffs as the EU) but not be part of the single market — Turkey has this arrangement with the EU. Conversely, you can be a member of the single market but not the customs union — Norway has this arrangement with the EU.

- **European Economic Area (EEA):** An agreement that allows some non-EU countries to participate in the EU single market. The EEA is made up of all the EU countries, plus three extra countries: Norway, Iceland, and Liechtenstein.

- **European Free Trade Association (EFTA):** A free-trade area comprising four countries: Iceland, Liechtenstein, Norway, and Switzerland. It ensures free trade and economic integration between members, but it also has close ties with the EU. EFTA members participate in the EU single market and Schengen, but are not part of the EU customs union.

- **Soft Brexit:** The term used for a future relationship in which the UK and EU remain closely aligned, perhaps by the UK remaining in the single market or customs union or both. Supporters of a soft Brexit argue that such a scenario would minimize disruption to businesses.

- **Hard Brexit:** The term used to signify more of a "clean break" with Europe, that would see the UK out of the EU, the single market, and the customs union — thereby leaving the UK free to negotiate its own trade deals and external tariffs with other countries. As negotiations wore on, *hard Brexit* also became synonymous with *no-deal Brexit*. Which brings me to. . . .

- **Brexit deal:** The Brexit withdrawal agreement (see Chapter 3), which sets out the terms for an orderly departure from the EU, including a transition period.

- **No-deal Brexit:** The UK leaving the EU without signing off on the withdrawal agreement, thereby ending free movement and participation in the single market and customs union overnight, with no transition period, which many people have argued could cause major disruption to businesses.

- **Article 50:** The clause in the EU's constitution that sets out the path for member states to leave the EU. For the UK to formally start the process of leaving the EU (incidentally, the UK is the first independent country ever to decide to leave the EU), it had to trigger Article 50.

- **Irish backstop:** It's complicated, and I recommend you turn to Chapter 3 for a more detailed explanation. But, put very simply, the backstop is an insurance policy in the withdrawal agreement that aims to avoid a hard border between Northern Ireland (which is part of the UK) and the Republic of Ireland (which is part of the EU). The backstop means the UK and the EU would remain in a customs union until a formal trade deal is agreed on by the two parties — something that could take many years.

Breaking Down the Brexit Timeline

Although the UK voted to leave the EU back in 2016, so far, the Brexit process has taken longer than most people ever imagined — and, factoring in future trade negotiations, may not be properly concluded for years.

Interestingly, the word *Brexit* pre-dates the 2016 referendum by a few years — check out the sidebar "Where did the word *Brexit* come from?" to discover more.

The basic timeline is as follows:

June 23, 2016: The British public votes to leave the EU.

March 29, 2017: Prime Minister Theresa May (who took over after David Cameron quit in the wake of the referendum result) triggers Article 50, giving the UK two years to negotiate its exit from the EU.

April 18, 2017: Theresa May calls a surprise general election, hoping a big win will give her greater negotiating power with the EU. But her plan backfires, and the election (held on June 8, 2017) sees her Conservative party actually lose its majority. The Conservatives remain in power, just about, by forming a minority government with the Democratic Unionist Party from Northern Ireland, although May was politically weakened by the result.

June 2017: Three months after triggering Article 50, the UK formally begins negotiating the terms of its withdrawal with the EU. Read more about both sides' crack teams of negotiators in Chapter 3.

November 2018: The EU and the UK publish their draft withdrawal agreement and a non-binding political declaration on future EU–UK relations. Both are swiftly approved by EU27 leaders.

January 15, 2019: The UK Parliament finally gets to vote on whether to approve the negotiated deal (the original vote, scheduled for December 2018 was post-poned). The deal is rejected by an overwhelming majority.

March 29, 2019: Two years after Article 50, this is supposed to be the date that the UK actually leaves the EU. However, amidst chaotic scenes in the UK Parliament as the withdrawal deal was repeatedly rejected by Members of Parliament (MPs), Article 50 had to be extended and the UK's exit was postponed by a couple of weeks.

April 12, 2019: The new Brexit date . . . but not for long.

October 31, 2019: The new, new Brexit date, as agreed between the EU27 and the UK at an emergency summit on April 10, 2019. With no immediate solutions in sight, and both sides wanting to avoid a no-deal Brexit, the delay is inevitable. However, should May manage to get her deal through Parliament before October 2019, the UK will be able to leave early.

December 31, 2020: The transition period, as set out in the withdrawal agreement, ends. (Although, given the delay to Brexit, it's likely we may see the transition period change as well.) During the transition period, the UK is still bound by EU rules and is part of the single market; free movement of people, goods, services, and capital can continue as normal. However, the transition period is dependent on approval of the withdrawal agreement. (Therefore, a no-deal Brexit means no transition period.)

December 31, 2022: The transition period could be extended until this date, if both sides agree.

WHERE DID THE WORD *BREXIT* COME FROM?

In 2016, the year of the referendum, Collins dictionary named *Brexit* the "word of the year," due to the massive increase in use of the word. But where did the word come from?

Combining *Britain* and *exit,* the word *Brexit* was first used to describe the UK's potential departure from the EU way back in 2012, long before David Cameron confirmed he would be holding a referendum on EU membership.

The word was inspired by *Grexit,* the name given to Greece's possible exit from the euro single currency — a story that dominated news in Europe in 2012. (In the end, Grexit never came to pass, and Greece ended up staying in the eurozone.)

Taking inspiration from this, a man called Peter Wilding, founder of the British Influence think tank wrote in 2012 that, without a real push for Britain to lead in Europe, "then the portmanteau for Greek euro exit might be followed by another sad word, Brexit."

It took a little while for the word to take off. In fact, we nearly had *Brixit* instead of *Brexit;* a few news sources, including the *Economist* and the *Daily Mail* originally wrote about the potential for a Brixit instead of Brexit. In the end, though, it was the *exit* bit that swung it, and, by the year of the referendum, Brixit had long faded from memory and all anyone talked about was Brexit.

And in case you're wondering which side of the Brexit fence Wilding is on, during the referendum campaign itself, he campaigned for the UK to remain in the EU. In other words, we have a Remainer to thank for Brexit — well, the word, at least!

Turn to Chapter 3 to read more about the negotiation process, terms of the withdrawal agreement, and the chaotic parliamentary approval process. In Chapter 4, you can read more about the much-less-talked-about political declaration on future relations, and take a peek at how our future relationship might evolve.

Looking at the Key Elements of the Brexit Negotiations

The withdrawal negotiations between the UK and the EU seemed to go on forever, but really they're just the tip of the iceberg.

That's because the withdrawal agreement only covers the UK's *departure* from the EU. It doesn't agree on critical elements of the future relationship between the two, such as trade. The withdrawal agreement is purely about getting the UK out of the EU in an orderly manner. Trade negotiations — and agreements that cover cooperation in areas like security and defense — will not begin until *after* the UK has left the EU. This was a big area of misunderstanding for a lot of people, who assumed the "Brexit deal" was essentially a trade deal.

So, what does this orderly exit involve? To ensure the UK's exit would be as smooth as possible, the two sides negotiated the following key points as part of the withdrawal agreement (you can read more about these points in Chapter 3):

>> The *divorce bill,* or how much the UK has to pay to cover its existing commitments to the EU.

>> The *transition period* (also known as *implementation period*), which is designed to ensure a controlled transfer, and give governments and businesses time to prepare for life after Brexit.

>> The rights of EU citizens already living in the UK (and the rights of UK citizens living in the EU) to retain their residency status after Brexit. Also, that the free movement of people would continue until the end of the transition period. Theresa May had made it clear during negotiations that free movement of people would have to end after the transition period — it was one of her "red lines" that she refused to budge on.

>> The fact that the UK will have to abide by EU laws for the duration of the transition period — something that raised a lot of eyebrows among Brexiteers.

>> How to avoid a hard border between Northern Ireland and the Republic of Ireland. The withdrawal agreement includes a provision for a temporary customs union between the UK and the EU until a trade deal is agreed upon, and this is known as the *backstop.* This backstop measure proved extremely unpopular among Brexiteers (and even many Remainers), even though it was designed to prevent a hard border and protect peace on the island of Ireland.

The UK's ongoing relationship with the EU in areas such as trade is *not* part of the withdrawal deal because, at the time of writing, none of that has been negotiated yet. The political declaration (see Chapter 4) sets out a vague aim to agree on a trading relationship that's as close as possible, but it avoids any specific details.

Deal or No Deal? Brexit Goes Down to the Wire

Although the EU27 leaders signed off on the withdrawal agreement and political declaration, Theresa May had her hands full trying to get approval from the UK Parliament.

The original parliamentary vote, which was scheduled for December 2018, was postponed at the last minute when it became obvious that almost no one in Parliament was prepared to support the deal. The Irish backstop was the main objection for most people, amidst concerns that it could inadvertently trap the UK in a permanent customs union with the EU — without the option to withdraw from that customs union in the future.

REMEMBER

The vote eventually took place in January 2019, at which point the UK Parliament spectacularly rejected (by a record majority) the deal that May and her team had spent almost 18 months negotiating.

But, like a fading Hollywood franchise that refuses to die, Theresa May brought the withdrawal deal back for a second vote, and a third, both in March 2019. Both times, Parliament rejected the deal. With just a couple of weeks to go until the intended exit date, the UK was on the verge of crashing out of the EU with no approved deal, meaning no transition period and potential chaos for UK businesses.

The EU looked on open-mouthed as chaotic scenes unfolded in Parliament. Meanwhile, the British public (and their Parliament) split further into factions: Some wanted to leave the EU with no deal, some wanted to delay Brexit and start negotiations again, some called for Brexit to be canceled altogether (a prospect that the EU had paved the way for when it agreed that the UK could just revoke Article 50 without getting the EU's agreement), and many called for a second EU referendum.

REMEMBER

At this point, MPs voted to wrestle control of the Brexit process from Theresa May and her government, meaning they could begin to debate their own ideas on how to get Brexit done. Unfortunately, this didn't work out either — it became glaringly obvious that there was no consensus on how best to leave the EU. All sorts of options were proposed: Leave the single market but remain in the customs union, leave the customs union but remain in the single market, have a second referendum on whatever deal is agreed upon, have a nice cup of tea and watch *Killing Eve*. (Okay, I made that last one up, but you get the idea — it seemed everyone had a different idea on how best to proceed.) All options were rejected. So, they voted again. And all options were rejected again.

As one British newspaper put it at the time, MPs took back control of the Brexit process, only to discover that they didn't know what it was they wanted.

Amidst all the confusion, the EU took matters into its own hands and decided to extend Article 50 until April 12, 2019 — an extension of two weeks to help get something, *anything*, through Parliament. This short extension wasn't enough, though, and the EU and the UK then agreed on another extension, pushing the Brexit date back to October 31, 2019.

If this painful process proved anything (beyond the UK's incredible talent for comedy), it's that Brexit means different things to different people. Remember that the referendum was a simple in/out vote. People were asked, should the UK remain in the EU or leave? Those who voted leave weren't voting for a particular type of Brexit on the ballot sheet; they were just voting to leave. Therefore, some of those who voted out undoubtedly had a hard Brexit in mind, while others will have leaned more toward a softer Brexit and maintaining close ties with Europe.

Therefore, when politicians talk about Brexit being "the will of the people," what they're really doing is interpreting their own version of the referendum result in line with their political position on Europe. As such, "the will of the people" has been used as an argument for a no-deal Brexit by hardliner Conservatives. Meanwhile, the opposition Labour Party, has interpreted the "will of the people" as meaning a softer Brexit.

With such disagreement on Brexit, it's hard to imagine at this point how the UK government and Parliament will find a way through this mess and reach a consensus on what sort of Brexit is best.

At the time of writing, Theresa May and Jeremy Corbyn, leader of the Labour Party, have been engaged in negotiations to try to reach a compromise solution that can get through Parliament. This may involve plans for the UK to join a customs union with the EU. We've yet to see whether these discussions will get anywhere, and whether the UK Parliament will ever approve the Brexit deal, so that the UK can finally leave the EU. As of this writing, everything's still on the table, including the unlikely prospect of a no-deal Brexit, or the (arguably more likely) prospect of Brexit being delayed into 2020. As with everything about Brexit, it's a case of watch this space!

Read more about the twists and turns of the parliamentary approval process in Chapter 3.

How Businesses Reacted to the Brexit Decision

During the referendum campaign, Team Leave made some optimistic predictions about the UK's post-Brexit trading prospects. There were promises of swiftly agreeing on attractive trade deals with the EU, the United States, and other global players, with little disruption for British businesses. After all, while governments may talk about trade deals like they're badges to collect and show off, it's everyday businesses that benefit (or don't) from the trade deals that are agreed upon.

Meanwhile, Team Remain was quick to point out that not being able to trade smoothly with the EU would hit British businesses hard, because Europe is a major export customer for the UK. There were warnings of chaos at British ports and an overall negative impact on imports and exports.

REMEMBER

After the 2016 referendum result, and throughout the Brexit negotiation process and beyond, businesses and the organizations that support businesses in the UK reacted with some grim predictions and threats, including the following:

» Telecoms giant Vodafone warned it might move its headquarters out of the UK and into Europe. (At the time of writing, it hadn't made such a move, but the company made a big acquisition in Europe in 2018, when it acquired Liberty Global's cable network in Germany and Eastern Europe.)

» Jaguar Land Rover warned of potential job losses, which sadly came to pass in 2018 (1,500 job losses) and early 2019 (4,500 job losses).

» Airbus warned that it might pull its wing building out of the UK in the event of a no-deal Brexit, and branded ongoing Brexit uncertainty "a disgrace" in January 2019.

» Retailer John Lewis ended up in a public spat with then–Brexit Minister Dominic Raab when it said Brexit uncertainty and the devalued pound were contributing to poor trading results.

» Lloyds Banking Group (and many other financial services companies) secured a banking license in Germany, paving the way to turn its Berlin branch into a full subsidiary company after Brexit.

» Nissan confirmed that it wouldn't be building the flagship X Trail SUV at its Sunderland plant, as originally planned, and warned that continued Brexit uncertainty "is not helping companies like ours to plan for the future."

- » Dyson founder Sir James Dyson, who had openly backed leaving the EU, announced in January 2019 that, although manufacturing would stay in England, he would be relocating the company's headquarters from England to Singapore — which had recently signed a trade agreement with the EU.

- » Ferry company P&O re-registered its entire fleet of ferries under the flag of Cyprus as a direct result of concerns over Brexit.

- » Sony confirmed that it would be moving its European headquarters out of the UK and into the Netherlands.

- » Numerous other companies warned of potential price rises and delays as a result of Brexit.

In short, many business leaders felt that Brexit was a mistake for the UK. Whether they're right in the long term remains to be seen.

REMEMBER

In March and April 2019, as Parliament struggled to reach consensus on a way forward and the clock ticked down toward the original day of the departure, business associations reacted with increasing dismay and frustration, particularly at the lack of clarity on the UK's future trading relationship with the EU.

The director general of the Confederation of British Industry (which represents almost 200,000 UK businesses), described Westminster as a "circus" and said that "jobs and livelihoods" depended on finding a new approach.

Meanwhile, the director general of the British Chambers of Commerce warned that businesses in the UK were not prepared for the consequences of a "messy and disorderly exit" (exiting the EU without agreeing on a withdrawal agreement). He said, "Government agencies are not ready, many businesses are not ready, and despite two and half years passing since the referendum, there is no clear plan to support communities at the sharp end of such an abrupt change."

For non-British readers, I should point out that, by normally polite British standards, these quotes represent pretty stiff language!

REMEMBER

It's clear, then, that Brexit will have some impact on businesses, whether it's minor inconvenience or major upheaval. Therefore, all businesses should prepare for Brexit and assess the potential impact that Brexit may have on their operations.

Assessing the Potential Impact of Brexit on Your Business

Whatever happens with Brexit, whatever happens with any future trade agreement between the UK and the EU, business will continue. As with any business change, evolution or disruption, it's about finding ways to adapt, ride out uncertainty, and future-proof your business as much as possible.

REMEMBER

At the time of writing, we don't know for sure what the full impact of Brexit will be — depending on the type of business and industry you're in, your company may hardly be affected. Regardless, it's important to plan for potential changes or disruptions so that your company isn't caught unawares.

If you were around in the late 1990s, you might remember talk of the "millennium bug." We were all told our computers would stop working as the new millennium dawned, that public services would grind to a halt and planes would fall out of the sky. None of it came to pass. So, although I don't want to downplay very real Brexit concerns, I think it's important to maintain a level head and approach Brexit as you would any period of business change, evolution, or uncertainty.

In the following sections, I look at some of the key business activities that may be affected by Brexit.

Trading across borders

If your UK business trades with customers in the EU, you may need to consider things like the following:

>> Whatever happens, trade between the UK and the EU will continue, but it may be subject to tariffs on goods, increased paperwork, and customs checks. The processes for customs duties and value-added tax (VAT) payments on imports from the EU may also change.

>> If the UK exits the EU with a withdrawal deal, then UK–EU trade will continue as normal for the duration of any agreed-upon transition period. During the transition period, both sides will start to negotiate a longer-term trade agreement.

>> However, if the UK exits the EU without a withdrawal deal, or if the UK and the EU can't come to an agreement on future trade arrangements, then the UK will trade with the EU under World Trade Organization (WTO) rules.

>> The picture for services companies selling their services in Europe may be slightly more complicated, since the trading of services tends to rely on close regulatory compliance. So, the ability of UK service companies to easily do business in the EU will depend on what the UK and EU agree on as part of their trade negotiations.

Read more about these potential changes to importing and exporting, and learn how international trade deals work, in Chapter 5.

Dealing with logistics challenges

Increased paperwork. Customs checks at the border. Customs payments. All of these potential developments will inevitably lead to higher costs and logistics challenges for businesses. Some of the key logistics considerations include the following:

>> Goods may be subject to increased customs checks as they cross a UK–EU border.

>> We may see delays at UK ports (especially at busy, high-volume crossing points like Dover), which will mean it will take longer to transport goods in and out of the UK.

>> Warehousing is in higher demand as businesses look to stockpile goods in case of disruption.

>> Even if the UK exits with a withdrawal agreement and swiftly secures a free-trade agreement with the EU, it's still likely that border controls may change in one way or another.

>> What's more, there are still likely to be some teething problems as the UK and the EU adjust to their new relationship, so it's wise to prepare for some level of disruption to your supply chain.

Turn to Chapter 6 to read more about these and other logistics challenges —plus tips on taking the family car to Europe.

Managing the impact on employees and access to labor

Brexit will prompt a change in UK immigration rules, because one of Theresa May's "red lines" in the negotiations was the desire to end free movement between the UK and the EU. For those businesses that employ EU nationals or are dependent on short-term labor from Europe, this could cause problems. You may need to consider things like the following:

>> Your EU national employees will need to obtain *settled status* if they want to remain in the UK indefinitely after Brexit. Settled status is the name given to the government scheme that provides security for EU nationals living in the UK, allowing them to stay on indefinitely.

>> The UK government plans to allow unskilled workers from "low-risk countries" (likely to include all of the EU) to be allowed to come and work in the UK for up to 12 months without needing a visa.

>> However, in light of the devalued pound and uncertainty around Brexit, many European workers are choosing to earn their money elsewhere in Europe, leading some industries to voice concerns about access to labor in the future.

>> It's vital that you support your employees through any period of business uncertainty or disruption.

Turn to Chapter 7 to read more about these and other employment-related issues, including potential changes to employment law, making sure you have continued access to the labor you need, and tips on how to engage and retain your employees in times of disruption.

Looking at other considerations

There are all sorts of other business considerations that don't fall under the headings of people, logistics, and trade, but are nonetheless important for businesses. These include the following:

>> Potential impact on EU-based subsidiaries or branches

>> What happens to intellectual property after Brexit

>> What happens to environmental standards, product safety standards, and other legal or regulatory requirements that your business complies with

>> The need to take steps to retain any .eu domain names that your business has

>> The impact of Brexit on your General Data Protection Regulation (GDPR) practices

>> The need to review and update your business contracts

Delve into these issues in more detail in Chapter 8.

Planning for the impact on your business

Clearly, there are lots of things to think about when it comes to preparing your business for Brexit. That's why I provide some handy checklists of questions to ask yourself — a sort of Brexit impact assessment in simple list form.

Turn to Chapter 9 to start assessing your business and preparing for whatever may come your way after Brexit.

Looking to life after Brexit

This book isn't about scaremongering or fueling fears that business will grind to a halt after Brexit. Quite the opposite. I like to think that Brexit, like any period of change, has the potential to lead businesses to new market opportunities, fresh ways of thinking, and better ways of doing business.

However you feel about Brexit, it's not going away anytime soon. Considering future trade talks between the UK and the EU, Brexit may dominate the news for some time to come. For this reason, it's vital that UK businesses stay focused on, well, doing business.

That's why, in Part 4 of this book, I look ahead to life beyond Brexit. There, you can find tips on how to protect your business against Brexit uncertainty, my ideas on what sort of opportunities may lie ahead for British businesses after Brexit, and a list of key Brexit developments to keep an eye on in the future.

Chapter **2**

The Road to Brexit: The UK's Rocky Relationship with the EU

Just because you live next door to someone doesn't mean you're always going to get along. Sure, she lent you some coffee that time, but she also plays loud music at 4 a.m. The same is (sort of) true of the United Kingdom (UK) and Europe. They may be neighbors, but they haven't always enjoyed the easiest relationship.

REMEMBER

Many people believe that the catalyst for Brexit was the rise of nationalism and, in particular, the emergence of the Eurosceptic UK Independence Party (UKIP). But dig a little deeper and it's clear that cracks began to show many years before that.

So, to answer the question, "How did we get here?," we need to dust off the time machine, fire up the flux capacitor, and go further back in time — long before the referendum itself, and long before UKIP was even a twinkle in Nigel Farage's eye.

In this chapter, I explore the history of the UK's often troublesome relationship with the European Union (EU), and unearth some of the reasons why Europe is such a divisive subject among Britons.

From Empire to the Aftermath of World War II

Instead of covering centuries of European wars and conflict, which might, er, take a while, I'll begin my review of UK–Europe relations in the 20th century. And if you're wondering whether the UK and Britain are the same thing, check out the nearby sidebar "What's the difference between the UK and Great Britain?"

WHAT'S THE DIFFERENCE BETWEEN THE UK AND GREAT BRITAIN?

Throughout this book, you'll notice that I sometimes talk about the UK, and sometimes refer to Great Britain, and sometimes just England. They're not all the same thing, although the terms are often used interchangeably.

Great Britain is the collective name given to England, Scotland, and Wales — which are all separate nations that share the same island. The United Kingdom includes Great Britain (England, Scotland, and Wales) together with neighboring Northern Ireland. (Its full name is the United Kingdom of Great Britain and Northern Ireland.) In very simple terms, much of the time, the four nations operate as one country, the UK — but not when it comes to football (soccer) teams. That's why you might see England versus Wales in the World Cup.

Many people around the world use *England* as a substitute for the whole of the UK — but this is a surefire way to offend anyone from Scotland, Wales, or Northern Ireland! England, as a name, only refers to the country of England, which is just one composite part of the UK.

So, in this book, when I use the term *Great Britain,* I'm referring specifically to the island comprising England, Scotland, and Wales. And when I refer to the UK, I mean the nation as a whole, including Northern Ireland. To further confuse matters, most Brits simply refer to the whole of the UK as Britain (not Great Britain), and I do that occasionally as well!

The end of an empire

After building up a vast worldwide empire, particularly during the 19th century, things started to change for Britain in the 20th century. British colonies began to seek independence — and, closer to home, the sheer cost of maintaining an empire was becoming hard to swallow.

Added to this was the cost of fighting two world wars — plus the growing influence of the United States on the global stage in the wake of these wars. Bottom line? A new political environment was emerging and times were a-changin'.

India and Pakistan gained independence in 1947, and, over the following decade, many other nations sought their own independence. British rule of Palestine ended in 1948. Malaya declared its independence in 1957 after a violent uprising. And Ghana, the first black African nation to declare independence from colonial rule, followed the same year. It was the beginning of the end for the British Empire, and most of Britain's colonies in Africa and the Caribbean gained independence in the 1960s.

Decades later, the handover of Hong Kong in 1997 (at which point Hong Kong became an administrative region of China) was seen as the final nail in the empire's coffin.

Keeping Europe at arm's length

What does all this mean for the UK's relationship with Europe? With Britain's global rule on the wane and calls for a more united post-war Europe (not least from the United States), Britain found itself looking for a different kind of global power — developing the country's "special relationship" with the United States while seeking greater influence closer to home.

REMEMBER

Yet British distrust of Europe remained strong and the ghost of World War II loomed large in people's minds. The UK obviously played a prominent role in World War II, and experienced huge loss of life as a result. The idea of getting into bed with other European countries — not just Germany, but countries that sided with Germany, and countries that played a less active role in defending Europe — left a bad taste in the mouths of many.

However, there were other long-standing reasons for the UK's reluctance to embrace Europe. Coupled with the ghost of World War II was Britain's natural geography. Great Britain is an island, after all, separated from continental Europe. While the UK has always been technically "part of Europe," most Brits at the time (and even now you could argue) wouldn't call themselves "European." Europe was a foreign land, alien in so many ways. For the post-war British public, Europe may as well have been Bolivia. Or Mars.

EEC, EC, EU: WHAT'S THE DIFFERENCE?

The 1957 Treaty of Rome created the EEC, which was designed to encourage economic integration among the then six member states. This economic integration included:

- A *common market* (a free-trading community with no trade barriers)

- A *customs union* (where members can trade freely without tariffs, and all members agree to charge the same tariff on imports from outside the union).

With its focus on free trade and one single market, the EEC was also often referred to as the "common market." So, when people talk about the European common market/single market, they're really talking about the EEC.

But the EEC didn't stay the EEC forever. As more countries joined and European integration gained momentum, it was no longer solely about economic integration, but also about *social* integration. As a result, people began to drop the "economic" bit and just talk about the "European Community."

The EEC's name was formally changed to the European Community (EC) by the Maastricht Treaty in 1992, the same treaty that officially established the EU. (See the section "Things (Start To) Fall Apart: The United Kingdom and Europe in the 1980s and early 1990s," later in this chapter.)

Now, bear with me, because this is where it gets a bit confusing. . . .

The EC, with its drive toward social and economic integration, was a critical pillar of the EU. But it wasn't the only pillar — meaning the two names, EC and EU, aren't strictly interchangeable. There were two other pillars alongside the EC: the Common Foreign and Security Policy, and the Police and Judicial Co-operation in Criminal Matters. Together, these three pillars made up the EU.

Because the EU and the EC weren't technically the same thing, they had different statutes and decision-making rules, which was just plain confusing for everyone. So, in 2009, the Lisbon Treaty came into force. This amended the Maastricht Treaty and created one unified constitutional basis for the EU and its pillars. Everything, in effect, became the EU.

For more on the inner workings of the EU, see the sidebar "How does the EU work, and who pays for it?," later in the chapter. You can also read more about key EU jargon and definitions in Chapter 1.

REMEMBER

So, perhaps it was no surprise that, when six European countries (Belgium, France, Italy, Luxembourg, the Netherlands, and West Germany) signed the Treaty of Rome in 1957, Britain, notably, observed but didn't sign up. This treaty created the European Economic Community (EEC), which later formed a critical pillar of the EU — see the sidebar "EEC, EC, EU: What's the difference?"

When Britain later applied to join the EEC in 1961, France intervened and Britain's entry was denied in 1963. France objected again to Britain's entry in 1967. It seemed the distrust was mutual. Britain's distant attitude to the Continent (in which it saw itself as part of Europe but also completely separate) hadn't gone unnoticed. It would be a few more years before Britain was allowed in.

Flares and Friends: The UK and Europe Cozy Up in the 1970s

Watergate. The end of the Vietnam War. Glam rock and David Bowie. The Beatles split. Bell-bottom jeans. We've fast-forwarded to the 1970s, and it's an interesting time to be alive. This is the decade in which the UK really started to build closer ties with what would eventually become the EU.

(Of course, it wasn't the EU yet, it was still the EEC at this time. If you haven't already, check out the sidebar "EEC, EC, EU: What's the difference?" to get a handle on the various names and acronyms.)

Officially joining the club

REMEMBER

After the UK's initial attempts to join the EEC were refused in the 1960s, it finally became a member in 1973. The UK wasn't the only country allowed into the club; Denmark and Ireland joined, too.

Europe was prospering in the 1970s. So, too, was the idea of a federal, much more integrated Europe. Contrast this with life in the UK in the 1960s and 1970s: union strikes, power cuts, political uncertainty, and did I mention the blue jeans? The UK felt in decline compared to its newly prosperous, peaceful neighbors across the water. As the then Prime Minister Edward Heath said in the 1971 debates over EEC membership, "For 25 years, we've been looking for something to get us going again. Now here it is."

Pretty much immediately after joining the EEC in 1973, the UK's political woes got worse as it faced the enforced three-day week (a move to conserve electricity in the wake of the coal miner strikes) and high inflation. Where was the prosperity promised by politicians in the run-up to joining the EEC? The UK's closer relationship with Europe wasn't off to a great start.

REMEMBER

In 1975, under the new Labour government (which had been voted in the year before), the UK held a referendum to decide whether to stay in the EEC. The majority voted in favor, with 67 percent of voters opting to stay in.

Looking for greater influence in Europe

Germany and France were the powerhouses of Europe at this time — as they still are. However, the UK government had concerns about Germany and France taking control of the European movement and hoped that, by becoming members of the EEC, Britain could exert its own influence.

It worked, too, in a way. If the UK hadn't joined the EEC in 1973 — if it had never joined at all, in fact — would the EEC have morphed into the EU much sooner than it did? I think it probably would have, given the ambitions of major European players at that time. So, you could argue that, through its membership of the EEC and greater involvement in Europe, the UK put the brakes on the federal Europe project. Temporarily, at least.

HOW DOES THE EU WORK, AND WHO PAYS FOR IT?

The EU is a body made up of 28 European countries or "member states" (that's including the UK — it'll be 27 member states when the UK officially exits the EU). It's built upon four key principles, or freedoms: free movement of people, goods, services, and money across countries in the union.

All EU citizens have the right to work, live, study, shop, and retire in any EU member country, and they're entitled to equal treatment. So, in effect, the EU is seen as a single member state.

The EU consists of seven institutions or decision-making bodies:

- **The European Parliament:** This is the EU's parliamentary body. Members of the European Parliament (MEPs) are directly elected by EU citizens. The European Parliament shares legislative and budgetary power with the Council of the European Union.

- **The European Council:** Made up of the heads of state of each EU member country, plus the President of European Council and the President of the European Commission, this body sets the EU's overall political direction and priorities.

- **The Council of the European Union:** The European Parliament represents EU citizens, but the Council of the European Union represents EU member governments. It's where ministers from EU countries meet to discuss and adopt laws and coordinate policy.

- **The European Commission:** This institution proposes legislation, puts decisions into practice, and handles the day-to-day management of the EU. Each member state has its own Commissioner.

- **The Court of Justice of the European Union:** Also known as the European Court of Justice, this is the EU's judiciary. Its job is to ensure that EU law is applied and interpreted uniformly across the EU, and settle disputes between national governments and EU institutions.

- **The European Central Bank:** This is the central bank for the 19 (at the time of writing) countries that have adopted the euro currency.

- **The European Court of Auditors:** This body looks after the interests of EU taxpayers by acting as an independent external auditor for the EU's finances.

Phew, that's a lot of institutions, right? So, who pays for all this activity? All EU member states have to contribute to the EU's central budget, which funds EU policies, supports development in the EU, and pays for the administration of the EU. In very simple terms, how much each member chips in is calculated based on its VAT receipts, customs duties, and gross national income. Currently, Germany is the EU's biggest contributor, followed by France, the UK, and Italy.

Back in the 1970s, when the UK joined the EEC, 70 percent of the EEC's budget was being used to finance the Common Agricultural Policy (a system of farming subsidies and other farming programs). With its relatively small agricultural sector, the UK didn't receive much back in subsidies for the amount that it was contributing. And, at the time, the UK was one of the poorer members. Things were way out of balance.

This imbalance gave rise to what's called the *UK rebate,* a permanent mechanism for reducing the UK's ongoing contribution to the EU's budget. The UK rebate was negotiated by Margaret Thatcher and has been in place since 1985. However, in recent years, the rebate has come under growing pressure and some member states have called for it to be scrapped entirely.

Things (Start To) Fall Apart: The UK and Europe in the 1980s and Early 1990s

In the 1980s and early 1990s, the UK's initial optimism about Europe started to wane in some areas of the government and public.

Alarm bells start ringing in the 1980s

Margaret Thatcher successfully negotiated the UK rebate in the mid-1980s, which saw the UK claw back some of its sizeable contribution to the EU's budget. But this victory came at a price.

Thatcher's tough brand of negotiation and Marmite leadership style (no one's ever on the fence about that British food spread, Marmite — and the same could be said about Margaret Thatcher) rubbed European leaders the wrong way. Discussing the rebate, she said, "They say it's their money, and I say it's mine."

REMEMBER

Meanwhile, at home, some parts of the ruling Conservative party were growing more and more uncomfortable with the UK's relationship with Europe. (Interestingly, support for joining the EEC had originally been strong on the right, while, on the left, the Labour Party was largely opposed to joining. This sentiment would reverse somewhat over the years.)

This discontent grew worse in the late 1980s, when French socialist Jacques Delors became President of the European Commission and began loudly voicing his dream of a more federal, joined-up Europe. A big part of his vision for Europe included common policies and, wait for it, one single currency. . . .

REMEMBER

Many Conservatives were horrified by this idea of a more federal Europe. The UK had joined a common market, they said, not a European "superstate." This sowed the seeds for dissent in the Tory Party over the issue of Europe — something that still hasn't been resolved to this day, as Europe continues to divide the Conservatives.

Black Wednesday

As a federal Europe began to take shape, the UK joined the European exchange rate mechanism (ERM) in October 1990.

The *ERM* was a system for reducing variability in exchange rates to help stabilize currencies in Europe. Without getting too technical, think of it as fixed margins for currency exchange rates, with an upper limit and a lower limit — member states had to keep the value of their currencies within this predetermined range.

In practice, the ERM supported the buying and selling of European currencies, and the idea was that stronger European currencies would be sold to bolster weaker currencies. At this time, in the early 1990s, the British pound was one of the weaker European currencies. Selling the pound in large numbers would only weaken it further, and that's exactly what happened. . . .

This buying and selling of currencies came to a head on what became known as *Black Wednesday*. On this day, September 16, 1992 (which, as you can probably guess, was a Wednesday) the pound came under huge pressure from currency speculators — currency traders began selling large amounts of sterling, which caused the value of the pound to collapse.

The Bank of England was forced to increase UK interest rates to 10 percent, 12 percent, and even 15 percent in the space of just one day. Unable to stop the pound from falling below ERM thresholds, the UK withdrew from the ERM. At the time, this was considered a real low point in the UK's relationship with Europe.

Facing its own currency woes, Italy withdrew from the ERM the day after. The ERM in its original form had been proven vulnerable. Ultimately, this would lead to the demise of the ERM and the eventual introduction of the euro.

The Maastricht Treaty

The Maastricht Treaty, which formalized greater integration among EU member states, was drafted in December 1991 and signed by the then Prime Minister John Major on February 7, 1992 (months before the Black Wednesday crisis).

Over the years, there have been various amendments to the Maastricht Treaty, including the Treaty of Amsterdam in 1999, the Treaty of Nice in 2003, and the Treaty of Lisbon in 2009. (See the sidebar "EEC, EC, EU: What's the difference?") However, the Maastricht Treaty is what paved the way for the EU as we know it today, and gave the go-ahead to the creation of a significantly more unified Europe.

Critics of the EU see this as a key turning point in the UK's relationship with Europe. They believe that, by signing up to greater integration and granting greater power to the EU, the UK had effectively signed away control of its own country. Was this something that UK voters had signed up for when they went to the polls in 1975 and voted to remain in the EEC?

The increasing transfer of power

Since the signing of the Maastricht Treaty, there has been a gradual and growing transfer of power from individual governments across the EU to central EU decision-making bodies.

For example, as the EU's judiciary, the European Court of Justice can overrule UK law. Fishing is another key example of the UK butting heads with the EU and its member states. (Complaints of French fishing boats "pillaging" British waters. Spats on both sides about who's allowed to fish where, when, and how much. That's a very simplistic view of a big, complicated issue — someone, not me, could probably write a whole book on UK–EU fishing disagreements.)

Budget contributions and free movement of people have also been key areas of conflict. To read more about these issues, head to the section "Drawing the Battle Lines: Key Issues in the Brexit Referendum," later in this chapter.

Rising Euroscepticism from the 1990s Onward

Certain EU decisions are made on a unanimous basis, which effectively means EU member states have the power to *veto* or block decisions in areas like taxation, foreign policy, and the euro.

Over the years, the UK has used its veto to block certain EU decisions, particularly on the single currency. The UK had declined to adopt the euro when it launched in 1999 (showing again how the UK was part of Europe, but also separate, thanks very much). Tony Blair, who had swept to power in 1997 with a clear wish to adopt the euro and patch things up with Europe, later quietly shelved plans to adopt the single currency. Britain's economy was doing well enough without it.

Another prominent example of the UK pushing back against the EU, and the euro, came in 2011, when then Prime Minister David Cameron vetoed the Franco-German-led treaty to save the ailing euro — plans that many felt undermined British interests. Cameron's veto prompted some serious eye-rolling and tutting among other European leaders (who simply planned to create a new deal without the UK), but delighted the more anti-Europe sections of his own party.

REMEMBER

By this point, Europe had become a bitterly divisive issue for the Tories. Euroscepticism had been growing throughout the 1990s and beyond, really since the signing of the Maastricht Treaty. The political chasms were getting wider and wider.

Many issues were at the heart of this rising Euroscepticism, and I touch on some of the biggest in the section "Drawing the Battle Lines," later in the chapter. But among the main sticking points for Eurosceptics was this nagging feeling that membership of the EU was costing more than it was worth. In other words, rightly or wrongly, many felt the UK wasn't getting much back in return for its financial contribution.

When the UK joined the EEC in 1973, Britain was in a pretty sorry state and was famously dubbed "the sick man of Europe." By the 2000s, though, things had changed. Trade unions had been weakened, strikes were (largely) a thing of the past, industry had been privatized, foreign investment was increasing, London was Europe's premier financial center, and the housing market (indeed, the economy as a whole) was booming. Rightly or wrongly, there was a growing belief that Europe had a lot to learn from the UK, not so much the other way around. Full integration was looking more and more unlikely.

REMEMBER

Quietly, in the background, a small Eurosceptic political party called UKIP was gradually gaining momentum. It was formed way back in 1993 (founding members had been opposed to the UK signing the Maastricht Treaty) on the basis of one simple policy: to get the UK out of the EU. UKIP was by no means an overnight success. Although it won three seats at the European Parliament in 1999, the party didn't get a single MP elected to Westminster until 2014 (when Conservative defector Douglas Carswell became MP for Clacton). But, over time, the party certainly tapped into something deep in British voters. Anti-EU sentiment — indeed, a general distrust of mainstream politics — was growing.

Right, Lads, Let's Have a Vote

As Euroscepticism continued to grow in the UK, nationalist parties like UKIP grew in popularity. After being dismissed as a "one-issue party," UKIP had won a seat in the UK Parliament — and had clearly tapped into voter concerns around immigration and the concept of free movement. This was a huge wake-up call for the mainstream political parties.

TECHNICAL STUFF

What do people mean when they talk about "nationalism"? *Nationalism* promotes the interests of a particular nation (in this case, the UK) over and above other nations. Key to nationalist ideology is the concept of *sovereignty,* or the right of a nation to govern itself, without interference from external powers. So when people talk about the UK giving away its sovereignty to the EU, they're talking about power being transferred from Westminster (the seat of the UK government) to the EU.

In 2013, then Prime Minister David Cameron was desperate to take control of the nationalist agenda and settle the issue that was causing no end of trouble in his own party. He set out plans to hold an "in or out" referendum on EU membership, but remained pretty vague about the timings, except to reject the idea of an immediate vote.

REMEMBER

During the 2015 general election campaign, the Conservative manifesto included the promise of a referendum on EU membership. In other words, Cameron was saying, vote for me now, and I'll give you a vote on Europe. The move paid off for him in the short term, as he won the general election. But he lost the EU referendum a year later.

What he thought was a move to "put the issue to bed" once and for all (or, at least, once and for all for that generation), backfired spectacularly for Cameron. It turned out to be one of the most brutal referendums in UK history. And the very idea of a federal Europe came under intense pressure — following the Brexit result there was fleeting talk of Grexit and Frexit coming next, with Greek and French politicians mooting the idea of their own vote.

Sure, the referendum wasn't legally binding, but the Conservative party had committed to recognizing the final result and delivering the wishes of the people. David Cameron resigned (and was filmed innocently humming his way back to the front door of Number 10 like it was just another ordinary day). Theresa May took over from him, promised to deliver Brexit, and the rest, as they say, is history.

Drawing the Battle Lines: Looking at the Key Issues in the Brexit Referendum

Before I end this whistle-stop tour of UK–EU relations, let me take a moment or two to reflect on some of the key issues that came to the fore during the referendum campaign. Many of these issues run right to the heart of Britain's problematic relationship with the EU.

Britain's financial contributions to the EU

Central to the arguments of many Eurosceptics was the belief that the UK gave the EU much more, financially speaking, than it got back in return.

How much does the UK really pay in?

The UK's contribution toward the EU's budget changes each year. But, as an example, the UK made a gross contribution of £13 billion to the EU budget in 2017.

(Without the rebate, the UK's gross contribution would have come to more than £18 billion.) In return, the UK received around £4 billion in EU spending, making its net contribution around £9 billion.

Remember that famous bus from the referendum campaign with the slogan on the side claiming that the UK sends £350 million a week to the EU? That figure excluded the rebate and the money the EU gives to the UK for public projects and funding.

The UK also benefits from EU membership in ways that are much, much harder to estimate, including increased flow of investment, and the ability to buy and sell products easily within the EU.

REMEMBER

But, yes, the UK does contribute more to the EU budget than it gets back. In fact, the UK is one of the biggest contributors in the EU. Much has been said about the fact that the UK contributes more to the EU budget than 26 other EU members combined. And this statistic is true. But perhaps a less emotive way to look at it is this: According to Full Fact (www.fullfact.org), in 2017, the UK's net contribution totaled 18 percent of all net contributors.

From a completely neutral standpoint, it makes sense that richer countries in the EU will contribute more than the poorer members (who are net beneficiaries of EU money). But, still, it's a hard thing to sell to voters — particularly in parts of the UK that have struggled economically.

Feeling the squeeze

On top of this, we've seen a reduced UK rebate — as the UK prospered, Tony Blair brokered a deal to give up some of its rebate — and calls from some EU members to scrap the rebate completely.

What's more, in recent years, the EU has moved to include sex work and sales of drugs in gross domestic product (GDP) calculations, which further boosts the UK's estimated contribution. (In 2014, the Office for National Statistics began adding up the contribution to the economy made by prostitutes and drug dealers — it came up with a figure of almost £10 billion!) As one newspaper headline put it at the time, the EU would be making the UK pay for our, er, bad habits.

TECHNICAL STUFF

GDP is the term used to describe the value of all the goods and services that a country produces in a given time (usually calculated annually). As a measure, GDP is used to indicate a country's prosperity and national development. You may also hear people talk about *GDP per capita*, which measures the ratio of GDP to the country's population.

To cut a long, and very complicated, story short, Eurosceptics were uneasy about the UK's significant contribution to the EU's spending pot, and questioning whether it was all worth it.

"Picking up the slack" for others?

Under EU rules, a member state's *budget deficits* (where spending is higher than revenue) must not exceed 3 percent of GDP. And *public debt* (government and public agencies' debt) must not exceed 60 percent of GDP. These rules are designed to ensure EU members manage their public funds in a sensible, sustainable way. That's the idea anyway.

The Italian government is (at the time of writing) going through a disciplinary process for falling foul of these rules, after reporting a deficit of 3.1 percent and public debt of more than 130 percent of GDP. To put that in context, the UK's deficit is 1.8 percent of GDP and public debt is around 87 percent of GDP — the latter being higher than the EU's threshold, but nowhere near as large as Italy's.

REMEMBER

This disparity across the EU is another major underlying factor in the UK's distrust of Europe. To some, it seemed the UK was picking up the slack or propping up countries that were not as fiscally responsible as others.

Immigration and free movement of people

Many Remainers suggest that immigration was behind the UK public's decision to vote "out." It wasn't the only issue, but public opinion appears to show that it was one of the key factors.

But, for some reason, the issue seemed to catch the mainstream political parties by surprise — even though the growing backlash against the idea of free movement was plainly obvious to anyone who read the newspapers or listened to the average conversation on the high street in the run-up to the referendum.

To stem the negative tide, before the referendum, David Cameron tried to negotiate a "handbrake" system for the UK benefits system. This system would have denied EU migrants full benefit entitlements for a set period of time after they arrived in the UK, and was designed to combat sentiment that too many EU migrants came to the UK to claim benefits. However, EU leaders believed this system went against the principle of the free market, and the idea was rejected.

Not only did large sections of the UK media portray EU migrants as coming for the benefits, but it also portrayed them as "pinching British jobs." The two fears aren't exactly compatible — are migrants coming to live off welfare or to steal people's jobs, which is it? — but it goes to show how Brexit is such an emotive issue for Brits.

REMEMBER

Ultimately, the overwhelming sentiment from much of the media was that EU migrants were a "drain on the system." Yet, official government figures show that EU migrants are in fact *net contributors* to UK finances, meaning they pay more in taxes than they take out in terms of public services (like healthcare, education, and so on). In fact, an Oxford Economics study found that the average EU migrant contributes £2,300 more to the public purse each year than the average British adult. In other words, EU migrants living in the UK more than pay their way.

The tricky issue of trade

Opinions and statistics regarding UK–EU trade will vary depending on who you talk to, and in fact the UK and EU calculate export trade differently (which is help-ful of them).

REMEMBER

One thing is clear, though: The UK runs a *trade deficit* with the EU as a whole, which means the UK imports more goods and services from the EU than it exports to the EU. In 2017, UK exports to other EU countries totaled £274 billion while imports from the rest of the EU into the UK totaled £341 billion. Those figures are based on Office for National Statistics data — the EU calculates imports and exports slightly differently.

Depending on which source you look at, between 8 percent and 18 percent of EU exports arrive in the UK. Meanwhile, UK exports to the rest of the EU come to well over 40 percent of total UK trade. This means the UK is heavily reliant on the EU as a trade customer.

REMEMBER

On the other hand, a staggering 23 member states have a trade surplus with the UK — which means they export more to the UK than they import from the UK. Germany and Spain are the biggest EU exporters to the UK. On that basis, Eurosceptics argue it's in the EU's best interest to negotiate a trade deal with the UK as soon as possible. (Read more about the negotiation process and what will happen with trade in Chapters 3 and 4.)

There's also the issue of financial markets. As a leading worldwide stock market, London is key to Europe's money markets and commodities, and many European companies have loans that are financed through London. Quite what will happen when these loans are due to be refinanced remains to be seen. But if a workable solution isn't reached, it will impact not only the London financial market, but also European money markets and everyday European businesses.

UK sovereignty

Slowly but surely, more and more power has been transferred from EU member states to Brussels. As an example of this, the European Court of Justice has dealt a number of hammer blows to the UK government with various policies being ruled illegal.

REMEMBER

A key argument of Eurosceptics was that the British public never voted to join a federal Europe, where the UK's laws would be dictated by the EU. Nor did they agree to the European Parliament having the final say on policies passed by the UK Parliament. The UK joined an economic union, not a social and political union. If the people voting in the 1975 referendum had known they were ultimately voting to stay in a federal Europe, would the result have been different? Quite possibly.

A big part of the problem lies with the politicians, here — specifically, a lack of honesty on where Europe was going and what it would mean for UK sovereignty. In his 1971 white paper on joining the EEC, then Prime Minister Edward Heath promised "no erosion of essential national sovereignty." Yet, in 1972 the UK Parliament passed the European Communities Act, which accepted the supremacy of EU law.

I guess you could argue Heath's word *essential* leaves some wriggle room, but, to the voting public decades later, it seemed like the wool had been pulled over a lot of people's eyes.

Divided kingdom? How the referendum results played out across the UK

The UK's constituent countries voted quite differently in the referendum. Table 2-1 breaks down the results by country.

TABLE 2-1   UK Countries Brexit Vote Results

Country	Percent Voting to Leave	Percent Voting to Remain	Result
England	53.38%	46.62%	Leave
Scotland	38%	62%	Remain
Wales	52.53%	47.47%	Leave
Northern Ireland	44.22%	55.78%	Remain

REMEMBER

Devolved parliaments in Scotland and Wales (even though Wales voted to leave as a nation) have been highly critical of the move to leave the EU, and the ruling Scottish National Party (SNP) government in Scotland has been trying to use the result to push for another Scottish independence referendum.

The situation in Northern Ireland is slightly different, with the ruling Democratic Unionist Party siding with the UK government on Brexit (even though the public in Northern Ireland voted to remain). And despite the fact that the Welsh population voted to leave, the Welsh devolved parliament is siding with its Scottish counterpart on a remain policy. Isn't politics fun?

In any case, what this will ultimately mean for the United Kingdom as whole remains to be seen. For now, the jury's out, and we'll wait to see if a Scottish independence vote does materialize. You can read a little more about Scottish independence in Chapter 12.

Meanwhile, what did the EU make of all this?

Like many in the UK, prior to the referendum result, EU officials generally felt there wasn't a chance in hell that the British public would vote to leave the EU. Secure in this belief, the EU itself took quite a backseat role in the referendum, doing little to play up the benefits of EU membership or counteract claims from Leave campaigners.

Just like David Cameron, the EU was looking forward to finally resolving this nagging issue of a UK exit. The vote was supposed to kick the subject into the long grass so that everyone could get back to the business of governing. But things didn't exactly pan out that way, and the UK's tumultuous relationship with the EU was reaching its painful, drawn-out climax.

2

Breaking Up Is Hard to Do

IN THIS PART . . .

Understand the negotiation process between the United Kingdom and the European Union.

Anticipate the United Kingdom's long-term relationship with the European Union.

Chapter **3**

Negotiating the UK's Exit from the EU

n June 2017, following the 2016 Brexit referendum result, the United Kingdom (UK) and the European Union (EU) formally began negotiating the terms of the UK's exit from the EU. This was a smooth, swift process where everyone got along brilliantly and unanimously agreed on what was best for both sides. I'm kidding, obviously. The discussions went on for almost 18 months and were hindered by several changes in personnel on the UK side.

REMEMBER

The fruit of these drawn-out negotiations is the *Brexit withdrawal agreement*, which was published in November 2018. (The agreement's official title is "The Draft Agreement on the withdrawal of the United Kingdom of Great Britain and Northern Ireland from the European Union and the European Atomic Energy Community" — a title so long-winded it makes you wonder whether its authors were being paid per word!)

In this chapter, I briefly set out who was responsible for negotiating the deal and break down the key terms of the withdrawal agreement. I also look at the painful process of trying to get the UK Parliament to approve the withdrawal agreement. But first, it's important to be clear on what I mean by "withdrawal agreement."

Understanding the Scope of the Withdrawal Agreement

The objective of the withdrawal agreement is to "ensure an orderly withdrawal of the United Kingdom from the Union." In order words, it only covers the Brexit process itself, including the following:

>> How much the UK has to pay to cover its agreed commitments to the EU (commonly called "the divorce bill")

>> A transition period to ensure that the exit is as smooth as possible

>> The rights of EU citizens already living in the UK (and vice versa)

>> What happens to the border between Northern Ireland and the Republic of Ireland in the short to medium term

I talk more about these terms in the section "Exploring the Draft Withdrawal Agreement" later in this chapter.

REMEMBER

A common misconception is that the withdrawal deal agrees the UK's relationship with the EU for the long haul, but that's not the case. It doesn't agree trading terms, for instance. All it does is pave the way for the UK to leave the EU in a way that's as orderly as possible. It's the Brexit equivalent of giving your employer two weeks' notice, as opposed to storming out of the office yelling, "I quit, losers!"

REMEMBER

The UK's ongoing relationship with the EU (including trade) is *not* part of the withdrawal deal because, at the time of writing, none of that has been negotiated yet. The really hard work begins after Brexit because that's when the UK formally begins negotiating, well, *everything else.*

So, when you hear people talking about Brexit exhaustion, and being sick of hearing about "the deal", you may want to break it to them (gently, maybe from a safe distance), that post-Brexit negotiations will probably go on for many years. As an example, Canada's trade deal with the EU took seven years to complete. Everyone hopes that the UK–EU trade deal will be wrapped up quicker than that, but there are no guarantees.

Finally, although the long-term relationship between the UK and the EU hasn't formally been agreed yet, it's worth noting that the two sides have come up with a non-binding political declaration that outlines (in vague terms) how they would like to see the relationship develop. You can read more about this declaration in Chapter 4.

The A-Team? Introducing Each Side's Negotiating Team

Boxing had the "Thrilla in Manila" and "Rumble in the Jungle." Brexit had the equally exciting (if you like political negotiations, that is) "Tussle in Brussels."

In this section, I take a look at the British and European teams charged with negotiating the UK's exit from the EU, and highlight some of the key things they said before, during, and after the difficult negotiating process.

REMEMBER

Naturally, these two negotiating teams each set out with very different goals in mind. The UK team was out to secure the best deal possible for the UK, but the EU team couldn't risk going too easy on their British counterparts. The EU had to send a stern message to the 27 other EU member states (now commonly referred to as "the EU27") — namely, that leaving the EU has serious consequences.

On the UK team

Remain-supporting Theresa May managed to cling to her role as prime minister throughout the withdrawal agreement negotiations, but there were a number of changes to the UK negotiating team.

Here are the major players on the UK side:

>> **Theresa May:** As prime minister, May had effectively been head of the UK Brexit negotiations since day one. But as time went on, her role became increasingly hands-on as various UK negotiators came and went. Best Theresa May quote? The immortal "Brexit means Brexit," repeated over and over again like a yogi's mantra.

>> **David Davis:** Initially appointed secretary of state for exiting the European Union to appease the hardline Brexiteers in the Conservative Party, Davis fell on his sword in July 2018. Best quote? The enigmatic "Nothing is agreed until everything is agreed."

>> **Dominic Raab:** Replacing David Davis in July 2018, Raab remained Brexit secretary until the negotiations were concluded in November 2018 — at which point, he promptly quit in protest over the deal he'd helped negotiate. (How big a role he played is up for debate. Many speculated that he was Brexit secretary in name only, because Theresa May effectively took back control of negotiations.) Best Raab quote? In his resignation letter, he wrote "I cannot reconcile the terms of the proposed deal with the promises we made to the country. . . ."

>> **Stephen Barclay:** Appointed as Brexit secretary one day after Raab's resignation, Barclay's role was said to be more focused on domestic preparations, now that UK–EU negotiations on the withdrawal deal had been completed. Key quote? Referring to the withdrawal deal he issued a firm, "This is the only deal on the table."

>> **Oliver Robbins:** Robbins has been a constant presence as Theresa May's Europe adviser, and was closely involved in negotiations. Best quote? As a behind-the-scenes operator, there are none. However, the *Telegraph* described Robbins as "the unelected civil servant who has usurped the Brexit secretary and seized control of the negotiations," which sounds a bit sinister.

>> **Sir Tim Barrow:** As Britain's ambassador to the EU, Barrow has been an important link between the two parties. Like any good diplomat, Barrow has wisely kept his mouth shut in front of the cameras, but he did hand-deliver Theresa May's formal Article 50 letter to the EU in March 2017.

On the EU team

The UK's Brexit secretaries came and went like buses, but the EU's negotiating team remained as steady and constant as the sunshine in Tenerife. Let's look at the key players on the European side:

>> **Michel Barnier:** The appointment of Barnier — a fan of greater European integration — as chief negotiator for the EU showed that the UK could expect no favors from the EU. Best Barnier quote? "There are extremely serious consequences of leaving the single market, and it hasn't been explained to the British people. We intend to teach people what leaving the single market means." He also famously said, "I can't negotiate with myself," when negotiations still hadn't started three months after Theresa May formally triggered Article 50 (see Chapter 1 for a breakdown of Brexit and EU terminology, like Article 50).

>> **Donald Tusk:** As president of the European Council, Tusk has been extremely vocal about the UK's decision to leave the EU. Best quote? Hard to choose between "I have been wondering what the special place in hell looks like for those who promoted Brexit without even a sketch of a plan how to carry it out safely" and "Brexit will be a loss for all of us. There will be no cakes on the table. For anyone. There will be only salt and vinegar." In a softer moment, he also said, "We already miss you," when he was handed the Article 50 letter.

>> **Jean-Claude Juncker:** The president of the European Commission has also been vocal about his thoughts on Brexit. Best quote? Speaking of the UK's

reluctance to pay the "divorce bill," he said "If you are sitting in the bar and you are ordering 28 beers and then suddenly some of your colleagues [are leaving without] paying, that is not feasible. They have to pay. They have to pay."

Other EU representatives, including Guy Verhofstadt and Antonio Tajani, received little press coverage during the negotiations.

Exploring the Draft Withdrawal Agreement

After lots of back and forth (and, presumably, lots of Eurostar sandwiches), the negotiating teams concluded their discussions, and the withdrawal agreement setting out the UK's "orderly" departure from the EU was published in November 2018.

At almost 600 pages, the withdrawal agreement makes a great doorstop, but not a very quick read! In this section, I pull out the most relevant details of what was agreed between the UK and the EU.

It's going to cost how much?

In the early days of the Brexit withdrawal negotiations, much of the focus and anger within the UK revolved around the so-called "divorce bill." As negotiations wore on, and especially after the draft agreement was published, attention switched largely to the Irish border issue (which I get to later in this chapter).

REMEMBER

The *divorce bill* refers to the amount that the UK will pay to the EU to cover obligations that it agreed to as a member state. In other words, it settles the UK's account with the EU and clears the slate for the future.

No specific figure appears in the withdrawal agreement, but the divorce bill is expected to be around £39 billion, payable over a number of years. In fact, the Office for Budget Responsibility estimates that the UK will be paying this until 2064, although most of it will be paid off by 2021. Part of this divorce bill will cover the UK's financial contribution to the EU budget during the transition period. (I talk more about the transition period next. Circle back to Chapter 2 for more about EU budgets and the UK's financial contribution.)

I know what you're thinking — £39 billion is quite an expensive divorce, right? It is, especially when you consider the schools budget for 5- to 16 year-olds in England in the fiscal year 2017–18 was also budgeted at £39 billion. (*Remember:* That's one year, though, whereas the UK will be paying the divorce bill over several years.)

Many Brexiteers insisted that the UK doesn't legally have to pay anything to the EU in order to leave, while others paint the divorce bill as being like an "entry fee" for access to the single market further down the line. Either way, the UK has repeatedly confirmed its commitment to settling its account with the EU, and that commitment was cemented in the final withdrawal deal.

Transitioning smoothly with the "transition period"

When the UK finally exits the EU, the idea is it will enter a transition period, and this transition period is a key part of the withdrawal agreement. (If the UK leaves the EU without signing off on the withdrawal agreement — otherwise known as a *no-deal Brexit* — there will be no transition period at all.)

The *transition period* (or *implementation period*) runs from the day the UK exits the EU, until December 31, 2020 (at the time of writing). The idea behind the transition period is to ensure a controlled transfer, and to allow businesses, government agencies, financial institutions, citizens, and others time to prepare for changes in how the UK deals with the EU after the transition period is over.

Especially with the UK's exit being delayed from March 29, 2019, until October 31, 2019 (more on the delay coming up later in the chapter), there's a strong chance that the transition period may also be extended. Many people agree that the proposed transition period probably won't be nearly long enough to negotiate a UK–EU trade deal, let alone other key aspects of the future relationship). If the UK and EU agree, the transition period could be extended until December 2022. This is one of the many as-yet-unresolved issues surrounding Brexit (turn to Chapter 12 to read about other unresolved Brexit issues to keep an eye on).

The obvious upside of the transition period is that it buys everyone time to prepare and paves the way for a smoother exit (as opposed to a cliff-edge, no-deal Brexit). It also gives the UK continued access to the single market and customs union for the duration of the transition period, and ensures that the UK has continued access to key European databases that are vital for security and law enforcement purposes. However, critics are quick to point out that it ties the UK to EU control for several more months, and possibly even longer than that.

What do these critics mean by "EU control"? Well, under the terms of the withdrawal agreement, during the transition period, the UK will:

>> Be legally obliged to abide by all EU rules (more on this coming up next in the chapter)

- » Lose membership of all EU institutions (so, in other words, the UK will have to abide by EU rules without having a say in the decision-making process for those rules)
- » Continue to pay into the EU budget
- » Be obliged to make extra financial contributions over and above the divorce bill if the transition period is extended

For these reasons, the transition period raised alarm among hardline Brexiteers, who were quick to point out that, instead of "taking back control" the UK government was still ceding control to Brussels.

Abiding by EU laws

The fact that the UK will have to abide by all EU laws for the duration of the transition period was one of the more eyebrow-raising issues of the withdrawal agreement (the divorce bill and Northern Ireland backstop being other key bones of contention).

REMEMBER

During the transition period, the UK will still be under the jurisdiction of the European Court of Justice, meaning the EU will continue to influence the UK's laws for the immediate future. But that's only if the UK exits under the terms of the withdrawal agreement — in the less-likely event of a no-deal Brexit, there will no transition period at all.

One potential problem arising from the transition period is that UK businesses may have to abide by a lower value-added tax (VAT) threshold, if proposed EU VAT changes come into force during the transition period.

WARNING

At the time of writing, UK businesses are exempt from paying VAT if their turnover is less than £85,000. But under proposed changes to the EU's VAT directive, this threshold would be set at €85,000 (which is around £76,000). This means that, for the duration of the transition period, UK companies would have to abide by the reduced threshold — a move that could force hundreds of thousands of small businesses to charge VAT for the first time.

This is just one example of the disadvantages the UK faces during the transition period by not having a say on EU rules and regulations. As a member of the EU, the UK was always able to block proposed changes in the VAT threshold. This veto — indeed, any meaningful role in decision making — will be lost on the day the UK exits the EU.

Formalizing citizens' rights

Around 3.8 million EU citizens live in the UK, and around 1.3 million Brits live in EU countries. For those European citizens living in the UK and Brits living in Europe, Brexit has brought a lot of anxiety; people who have built lives for themselves in a new country were understandably worried about their right to stay on after Brexit.

Business as usual — at least for now

Establishing citizens' rights was one of the top priorities for both the UK and EU teams — and, broadly speaking, was one of the easier things to agree on. In simple terms, the EU agreed to offer UK citizens the same rights as the UK offers to EU citizens. Quid pro quo.

REMEMBER

What does this mean in practice? Again, it all depends on whether the UK exits the EU in an orderly way, by approving the withdrawal agreement, which is far from guaranteed at the time of writing. For now, let's look at what the withdrawal agreement has to say about citizens' rights:

>> EU citizens already living in the UK will retain their residency and social security rights after Brexit.

>> UK citizens already living in an EU country will also retain their residency and social security rights after Brexit.

>> Free movement of people from the EU to the UK will continue until the end of the transition period, whether that's December 31, 2020, or a later date.

>> EU citizens who move to the UK before the end of the transition period will be able to stay in the UK indefinitely under the government's "settled status" scheme. They'll have broadly the same rights as before (including being able to have close family members come and live with them), providing they don't leave the UK for a period of five consecutive years.

>> Likewise, UK citizens who take up residency in the EU before the end of the transition period will also have the right to remain indefinitely, so long as they don't leave the EU for a period of five consecutive years.

>> Anyone who stays in the same EU country for five years or more will be entitled to apply for permanent residency.

Read more about settled status, citizens' rights and how they relate to employing EU citizens in the UK in Chapter 7.

What's not yet clear for UK citizens living in an EU country is what happens if they later decide to live and work elsewhere in the EU. For example, a UK citizen living and working in Germany will retain the right to stay on in that country. But what happens if he wants to move to Spain in 2025? His German residency doesn't guarantee him the right to live and work elsewhere in Europe — that's reserved for EU citizens only.

The end of free movement from the EU to the UK

Free movement of people is one of the key principles of the EU, guaranteeing that any EU citizen has the right to live and work in any other EU country. In practice, this meant that the UK accepted workers of all skill levels from the EU. Meanwhile, workers from outside the EU are accepted based on their skills. Some saw this as preferential treatment for EU citizens, resulting in too many unskilled workers coming to the UK — which is perhaps why free movement became such a critical part of the referendum campaign (see Chapter 2).

REMEMBER

After the transition period is over, Theresa May has made it clear that this free movement from the EU to the UK will end. The EU has accepted the UK's intention to end free movement after 2020 (or whenever the transition period ends), and this has been written into the political declaration on future relations between the EU and the UK — read more about this declaration and the future relationship in Chapter 4.

So, free movement as we know it will come to an end after Brexit (well, after the transition period, assuming there is one) but the specific terms of this arrangement — how it'll work in practice in the long term — have yet to be negotiated.

REMEMBER

After the transition, EU citizens looking to live and work in the UK will, in theory, be covered by the same immigration policy that applies to migrants from outside the EU. At the time of writing, the UK government is considering implementing five-year visas for skilled migrants with a minimum salary of £30,000, although this plan has met with some opposition. Either way, Theresa May has made it clear that she wants an immigration system based on skills, and that EU citizens will not get preferential access over migrants from the rest of the world.

That's all well and good, but what about UK industries and businesses that rely on unskilled labor from the EU? In December 2018, the government released its post-Brexit immigration plans, and these included a special exemption for low-skilled workers from "low-risk countries" (which is likely to include EU countries).

Under this "temporary worker" scheme, low-skilled workers will be able to live and work in the UK for up to 12 months without having to apply for a visa. These temporary workers won't be able to bring their family members to live with them, access public funds (such as benefits), or apply for permanent residency while they're working in the UK.

The government also said it would be testing a specific scheme for agricultural workers in 2019, although there are no further details on this at the time of writing.

Why hasn't anything been agreed on trade yet?

So, what happens with trade, I hear you ask? This is the area that many UK businesses want clarity on, yet it remains one of the biggest uncertainties. Because the withdrawal agreement only covers the UK's exit from the EU, nothing concrete has been agreed on for trade beyond the transition period.

REMEMBER

According to the withdrawal agreement, the UK will remain part of the single market — with all the same rights to free movement of goods and services — for the duration of the transition period. So, until the end of December 2020 (or whenever the transition period is over), trade will continue as it did before Brexit.

This gives businesses some sense of stability and allows them time to prepare for future changes . . . when those future changes have been agreed upon.

REMEMBER

Effectively, the UK agreed to leave the EU without any certainty on what would happen with trade. The political declaration on future relations between the UK and the EU (see Chapter 4) sets out some vague intentions for a close trading partnership, but the specifics of that long-term trading relationship have yet to be agreed upon.

How did the UK get to the point of exiting the EU without any firm agreement on how it would trade with Europe? The short answer is, the UK didn't want to. Here's the slightly longer answer: Initially, the UK government was hoping to tie trade negotiations in with the withdrawal agreement. The EU, however, always saw withdrawal and future trade as two separate agreements. In other words, the EU said (and I'm paraphrasing here), "Nuh-uh, first you leave, then we talk trade."

In Chapter 12, I highlight trade as one of the key developments to keep an eye on as Brexit unfolds, and set out some potential scenarios for the UK's future trading relationship with the EU. You can also read more about the impact of Brexit on importing and exporting in Chapter 5.

Of course, one of the major stumbling blocks in delaying trade negotiations until after the UK has exited the EU is the impact this may have on the border between Northern Ireland and the Republic of Ireland. Which brings me to the next section. . . .

Northern Ireland and the tricky issue of the "backstop"

If you're living in the UK, you heard a lot about Northern Ireland and the "backstop" during the negotiations. In fact, the backstop became one of the major sticking points when the withdrawal agreement went before UK Parliament for approval. (See "Getting Parliamentary Agreement on the, er, Agreement," next in this chapter.)

But what is the backstop, and what does the withdrawal agreement mean for the frictionless border between the Republic of Ireland and Northern Ireland? Before I get to that, let's have a super-quick history lesson.

The Good Friday Agreement

Signed in 1998, the *Good Friday Agreement* (also known as the *Belfast Agreement*) helped to bring about peace on the island of Ireland and end what was known as "the Troubles," a decades-long conflict between the Unionists/Loyalists (who wanted Northern Ireland to remain part of the UK) and the Nationalists/Republicans (who wanted Northern Ireland to join a united Ireland). There was a whole lot of religious disagreement mixed in there, too — Unionists were mostly Protestant and Nationalists were mostly Catholic.

After decades of violent conflict (which spilled over into the Republic of Ireland and the island of Great Britain), the UK government, the Irish government, and various parties from Northern Ireland signed the Good Friday Agreement. (The United States also played a key role in the discussions.) This agreement created a devolved government in Northern Ireland (called the Northern Ireland Assembly), with the Unionists and Nationalists governing together in a power-sharing arrangement.

It wasn't all plain sailing from there; the Northern Ireland Assembly was suspended in 2002 for five years, and the power-sharing arrangement broke down again in January 2017, resulting in the Northern Ireland government being dissolved. At the time of writing, in April 2019, the two main parties in Northern Ireland had yet to reach an agreement and form a new government.

REMEMBER

What's all this got to do with Brexit? Well, a key part of the Good Friday Agreement is the complete removal of physical borders between Northern Ireland and the Republic of Ireland — as well as free movement across both countries. This is not just about making inter-island trade and travel easier; it's also about allowing closer ties between the communities and breaking down the barriers (physical and otherwise) to peace and stability.

However, this lack of border caused a major problem in the UK–EU negotiations. Why? Because no physical border between Northern Ireland (which is part of the

UK) and the Republic of Ireland (which is part of the EU) means no border between the EU and a non-EU country. The UK and the EU had to find a way to overcome this hurdle, without jeopardizing peace and stability on the island of Ireland.

REMEMBER

It's important to note that no one, including the EU, wants to see a hard border between Northern Ireland and the Republic of Ireland. No one is in favor of installing border controls. However, the EU obviously wants to protect its single market and customs union from the uncontrolled flow of goods — and it needs some form of customs control to do this. Meanwhile, the UK obviously wants to ensure that Northern Ireland isn't isolated from the rest of the UK, and that Northern Ireland doesn't return to conflict.

Various solutions have been proposed, including a border down the middle of the Irish sea, effectively separating Northern Ireland from the rest of the UK — an idea that angered the Democratic Unionist Party in Northern Ireland, prompting Theresa May to reject the proposal. The EU also proposed that Northern Ireland become part of a "common regulatory area" with Ireland, which would mean Northern Ireland being subject to different regulations than the rest of the UK — an idea also rejected by the UK government.

What the Brexit withdrawal agreement says

Until we know what the UK's future trade relationship will be with the EU, it's impossible to find a permanent solution to this problem. The border issue will, therefore, form part of ongoing negotiations between the UK and the EU.

REMEMBER

That's why the withdrawal agreement includes a provision for a temporary customs union between the UK and the EU until a trade deal is agreed (see Chapter 1 for a breakdown of EU and Brexit terms, such as *customs union*). This provision is known as the *backstop.* If the UK and the EU haven't agreed on a trade deal that avoids a hard border before the end of the transition period, then the backstop arrangement will kick in. In this way, the backstop is like an insurance policy.

The backstop arrangement is as follows:

>> Until a trade deal is agreed upon, Northern Ireland will be aligned to EU rules on issues such as food and the standard of goods. This would mean there's no need for border checks between Northern Ireland and the Republic of Ireland, because Northern Ireland would effectively be treated as part of the EU.

>> In theory, goods flowing from the rest of the UK into Northern Ireland (and vice versa) would be subject to checks and controls. However, the backstop allows for a *single customs territory* (basically, a temporary customs union) between the UK and the EU, which ties the UK to EU customs and control for the duration of the backstop.

>> As long as the backstop is in force, the UK will have to comply with "level playing field conditions," which are designed to prevent competitive advantage. For example, the UK wouldn't be able to implement any trade deal with non-EU countries that would involve removing tariffs on goods.

>> Neither party can unilaterally withdraw from this temporary customs union, meaning the UK can't withdraw from the backstop without EU approval. You can imagine how those in favor of Brexit feel about this!

WHAT'S GOING ON WITH GIBRALTAR?

As a British Overseas Territory, the Rock of Gibraltar (affectionately known as "The Rock," not to be confused with Dwayne "The Rock" Johnson) is owned by the UK but is self-governing. This tiny piece of land — less than 3 square miles — is attached to the mainland of Spain but is home to around 32,000 British citizens. Gibraltar is not just home to British citizens, though; it's also strategically important for the UK, with its UK military base and location just 12 miles from the coast of North Africa.

Spain ceded Gibraltar to Great Britain in 1713 and has wanted it back pretty much ever since. However, the people of Gibraltar have voted in two referenda (the most recent being in 2002) to remain under British rule.

In the Brexit referendum in 2016, the people of Gibraltar also voted overwhelmingly to stay in the EU, with a massive majority of 96 percent, yet, just like the rest of the UK, Gibraltar will no longer be part of the EU after Brexit.

This creates a bit of a headache for Spain, which has close economic ties with The Rock (again, the territory, not the former wrestler-turned-actor). Also, did I mention that Spain would like to have Gibraltar back, thank you very much?

This came to a head when the published withdrawal agreement included proposals to create working groups between London and Madrid to discuss the future of Gibraltar. The UK insisted that this wording was just about working out the technicalities of Brexit in Gibraltar (movement of goods and people and so on). But, to the Spanish government, the wording opened up a new opportunity to press for sovereignty over Gibraltar.

Things turned a little uglier when, in January 2019, Spain insisted that a footnote be added to straightforward EU legislation on visa-free travel for Brits popping over to Europe after Brexit. The footnote described Gibraltar as a "colony of the British Crown" and referred to "controversy" over its sovereignty. The UK government, the UK's ambassador to the EU, and the chief minister of Gibraltar strongly condemned this description and insisted that Gibraltar is not a colony.

WARNING

Here's the really big problem, though. The backstop is intended to be a temporary arrangement, with the above conditions, until a proper trade deal is agreed upon between the UK and the EU. However, if the UK and the EU can't agree on a trade deal, then the backstop would apply indefinitely. This would tie the UK to the EU single market, and EU control, indefinitely. Having no guaranteed end to the backstop is a huge concern for many people who voted to leave the EU.

You can see why the border was one of the toughest parts to negotiate in the draft agreement. And when the agreement was published, and people began to fully understand what the backstop might mean, that's when the fun really began. The backstop became one of the biggest talking points as the UK Parliament came to vote on the withdrawal deal.

As an aside, Gibraltar also briefly received a lot of attention when the withdrawal agreement was published. To find out why, check out the sidebar "What's going on with Gibraltar?"

Getting Parliamentary Agreement on the, er, Agreement

Although the Brexit withdrawal agreement was smoothly approved by the leaders of the EU27 (the 27 countries remaining in the EU), Theresa May faced an uphill battle getting the withdrawal agreement signed off by the UK Parliament.

At the time of writing, this battle is still ongoing and there's very little clarity on whether the UK Parliament will approve the withdrawal deal. This leaves the UK in an interesting position, because the EU has been very clear that it won't reopen negotiations on the withdrawal agreement — the deal on the table is the only deal on offer, so to speak. But let's take a look at Theresa May's efforts to get parliamentary approval on the withdrawal agreement she spent almost 18 months negotiating with the EU.

Voting on the withdrawal deal: Round 1

In the first instance, a House of Commons vote was scheduled for December 11, 2018, to approve or reject the agreement. But the day before the vote was scheduled to take place, May postponed the vote because it was becoming glaringly obvious that the deal would be rejected by a large margin.

REMEMBER

Although the vote was postponed, it was a case of delaying the inevitable; when the vote finally took place on January 15, 2019, the withdrawal deal was overwhelmingly rejected by a record majority: 432 votes to 202. In other words, it took a severe beating.

The backstop arrangement was a significant factor in Members of Parliament's (MPs') dislike of the withdrawal agreement, so, as the clock ran down and the leave date of March 29, 2019, fast approached, Theresa May repeatedly went back to the EU to try to secure legally binding assurances that the backstop wouldn't apply indefinitely. The EU was unwilling to put a time limit on the backstop or allow an exit clause for the UK to leave the backstop without EU approval.

These discussions went right down to the wire, as a second House of Commons vote to approve or reject the withdrawal deal was set for March 12, 2019 — just 17 days before the UK's original planned departure date of March 29, 2019. Talk about cutting it fine!

Immediately after postponing the vote in December 2018, Theresa May survived an attempted leadership coup by hardline Brexiteers. Although more than one-third of Tory MPs voted "no confidence" in her leadership, she won enough support to stay on as prime minister.

Then in January 2019, a day after the delayed withdrawal deal vote took place (and the deal was rejected), the opposition Labour Party mounted its own challenge to the government and tabled a "no confidence" motion (the first against a UK government for more than 20 years). This was rejected by 325 votes to 306, meaning the Conservatives clung on to power, just about.

REMEMBER

In addition, there was a lot of talk about holding a second Brexit referendum, commonly referred to by campaigners as "the People's Vote." Labour leader Jeremy Corbyn pushed for an early general election, with the idea that Labour could take power and negotiate a new deal with the EU. And the European Court of Justice ruled that the UK could just cancel Article 50 and remain a member of the EU without getting permission from the 27 other members. It was a busy time for political journalists, while the general population (both in the UK and across Europe) simply scratched their heads and wondered what on earth was going on (see the sidebar "Meanwhile, outside of Westminster . . ."). However, there was more turmoil still to come.

Voting on the withdrawal deal: Round 2

With rumors of key cabinet ministers resigning over the impending prospect of a no-deal Brexit, Theresa May was forced to soften her stance and offer MPs the chance to vote on a no-deal Brexit and the option to delay Brexit, as well as voting on her withdrawal agreement for a second time.

This happened as a series of three votes across three days:

>> On March 12, 2019, MPs voted overwhelmingly to reject the withdrawal deal again — this time by a margin of 149 votes.

>> Then, on March 13, 2019, MPs voted on whether to leave the EU without a deal. In a tight vote, MPs voted to reject a no-deal Brexit under any circumstances, by 312 votes to 308.

>> Finally, on March 14, 2019, MPs voted in favor of extending Article 50 and delaying Brexit. This delay was approved by a margin of 211 votes, giving Theresa May permission to ask the EU for more time to find a way forward.

More votes, and Brexit is delayed (for the first time)

Theresa May refused to give up on her withdrawal deal, even though MPs had already rejected it twice. But her plans to bring the deal back to Parliament for a third vote were hampered by John Bercow, speaker of the House of Commons, who, with just 11 days to go until the original exit date, refused to allow another vote on her deal, unless the deal itself had materially changed since the last time MPs voted on it (of course, it hadn't changed). This plunged the UK government into constitutional chaos, with no clear way forward in sight.

Meanwhile, the government and businesses around the UK were spending a fortune preparing for the potential chaos of a no-deal Brexit. Because, even though MPs had rejected the idea of a no-deal Brexit, a no-deal Brexit was the legal default scenario if the withdrawal agreement wasn't approved.

At this point, the EU then took matters into its own hands and moved the exit date back a couple of weeks to April 12, 2019, to give the UK more time to find a way forward.

MPs then held a series of votes in an attempt to find some sort of consensus. By this point, oddly, everyone had stopped talking about the withdrawal agreement, and had jumped ahead to debating options for the UK's future trading relationship with the EU, even though the EU had said trade could not be negotiated until *after* the UK had actually left the EU . . . which it couldn't do until it approved the withdrawal agreement. The UK had effectively become stuck in a Kafkaesque nightmare of fairly meaningless and repetitive votes, while the British public, and the EU, looked on in horror.

On March 28, 2019, MPs voted on a series of their own options or ideas for Brexit, all of which were rejected (some were rejected more narrowly than others). These options included:

>> **A plan for the UK to negotiate a permanent customs union with the EU (even though the idea of being trapped in a permanent customs union with the EU was the reason many people were enraged by the backstop):** Confusingly, this option came the closest to winning, in that it was rejected by just six votes.

>> **A plan for the UK to hold a second referendum, giving the public a chance to confirm or reject the withdrawal deal:** This also came pretty close; it was rejected by a margin of just 27 votes.

>> **A plan for "common market 2.0," whereby the UK would join the European Free Trade Association (EFTA; see Chapter 1) and the European Economic Area (EEA; again, see Chapter 1), to ensure continued access to the EU single market:** This would also mean accepting free movement of people — something that Theresa May had ruled out early in the Brexit negotiations. This, too, was rejected, by a margin of 95 votes.

>> **A plan for the UK to leave the EU with no deal (even though this had already been rejected previously — see what I mean about Kafkaesque!):** This plan was widely rejected, by a margin of 240 votes.

>> **A plan for the UK to just revoke Article 50 and forget about Brexit:** This plan lost by 109 votes.

Basically, Parliament held a lot of votes, and none of them got anywhere. It seemed politicians would never reach a consensus on how to "do" Brexit.

Voting on the withdrawal deal: Round 3

Theresa May did, in the end, get to bring her withdrawal agreement back to Parliament for a third vote — although the result was the same. On March 29, 2019 (the day the UK was originally supposed to be leaving the EU), MPs voted for a third time to reject the withdrawal agreement. This time the margin was much smaller — just 58 votes — but it was still a humiliating defeat for May, especially because she had promised to resign and give Conservative hardliners what they wanted (a new leader) in return for backing her deal. They still rejected it, leaving many unsure whether (or when) May would step down.

MPs then held a second round of votes on their own options, including the customs union, common market 2.0, and the second referendum. All options failed to gain a majority. Once again, all were rejected.

Theresa May then surprised everyone by inviting Jeremy Corbyn and Labour representatives to help find some sort of consensus on Brexit. At the time of writing, both May and Corbyn were still engaged in these negotiations, but few people have any real hope of these discussions bearing fruit. That's because the two leaders have such different views on how to proceed with Brexit.

Labour is in favor of joining a customs union with the EU, which would make UK–EU trade easier in future but would limit the UK's ability to do trade deals with non-EU countries. Theresa May, however, has been against the idea of joining a customs union with the EU. Labour's official policy supports the idea of a second referendum (even if Corbyn himself isn't personally that bothered about holding a second referendum). May, meanwhile, would face another revolt from her own party if she agreed to hold a second referendum. It seems unlikely that the Conservatives and Labour can reach an agreement on Brexit anytime soon.

Brexit is delayed . . . again

At an emergency EU summit on April 10, 2019, two days before the revised Brexit date of April 12, the EU27 met to decide just what to do about the UK — the country that had been desperate to leave the EU for years but couldn't quite figure out how to do it.

The EU and the UK agreed to delay Brexit again, this time until October 31, 2019. (Is it me or does the Halloween date feel appropriate?) However, this extension is flexible, meaning that in the unlikely event that Theresa May manages to get approval on her withdrawal deal before then, the UK can leave early.

This extension was absolutely necessary to avoid the potential chaos of a no-deal Brexit. But it meant the UK would be forced to participate in EU elections, scheduled for May 23, 2019. At the time of writing, the UK was preparing to take part in EU elections, and elect Members of European Parliament (MEPs).

So, what happens next?

Good question! No one really knows how Brexit will play out from here — whether May will ever get approval of her withdrawal agreement, whether the UK will decide to join a customs union with the EU, whether Brexit will end up being delayed again. . . .

Here are some potential outcomes that may happen before October 2019:

>> If May and Corbyn can reach an agreement, the political declaration on future relations (see Chapter 4) may or may not be revised to talk about joining a customs union with the EU. (Changes to the withdrawal agreement seem

unlikely, given the EU and Theresa May's insistence that the legally binding withdrawal agreement cannot be changed or renegotiated.) Parliament would then have the chance to vote again on May and Corbyn's agreed-upon approach.

>> MPs may hold yet more indicative votes on their own alternative approaches to Brexit.

>> We may see a second referendum, whereby the public votes on the withdrawal agreement and political declaration.

>> The UK may even hold an early general election. If Parliament continues to be deadlocked on all options, this outcome will become increasingly likely.

>> The UK could, in theory, still exit the EU without agreeing on a deal at all (no-deal Brexit), even though this has been strongly rejected by MPs. At the time of writing, no-deal Brexit remains the legal default if the UK doesn't approve the withdrawal agreement.

>> In theory, Brexit could just be canceled, prompting both cheers and outrage from the public, depending on their Brexit stance.

One thing is sure: It's going to be an interesting time as the UK prepares for the new exit date of October 31, 2019! And if none of these options happen, and no consensus is reached on a way forward, there's a very strong chance that Brexit will be delayed again.

MEANWHILE, OUTSIDE OF WESTMINSTER . . .

To outsiders, the political wrangling in Westminster looked about as dignified as a bunch of cats fighting in a sack. Meanwhile, out in the real world, business owners, property owners, investors, and anyone exchanging her hard-earned sterling for euros in time for her summer holiday were all noticing the very real effects of Brexit uncertainty.

In business, companies reported reduced foreign investment and concerns such as supply-chain interruptions, rising costs, and reduced access to unskilled labor. Many companies have simply been delaying major decisions and significant investment until the uncertainty is cleared up. What's more, companies have had to divert precious time and resources away from growing the business to dealing with potential Brexit implications, especially preparations for a disruptive no-deal Brexit.

(continued)

(continued)

Overseas companies with UK offices have also been getting cold feet, with companies like Sony and Panasonic moving their UK operations to the Netherlands (see Chapter 12). Nissan and Honda both confirmed in early 2019 that they would close plants in the UK, resulting in thousands of job losses. (Although, it's important to note that in both cases production is being moved back to Japan, not to an EU country. Thanks to Japan's new trade deal with the EU, the historic 10 percent tariff on Japanese car imports into the EU has been removed and replaced with a 0 percent tariff for eight years.)

The pound was hit hard, too. Immediately after the referendum result in 2016, the pound fell to its lowest level against the dollar since 1985. (The euro also suffered against the dollar as Europe woke up to the news that the UK would be leaving the union.) Almost £85 billion was wiped off the Financial Times Stock Index (FTSE) 100 after the result was announced.

However, since 2016, both the pound and the financial markets have recovered somewhat and been fairly stable — well, given the ongoing uncertainty. It's also worth noting that the International Monetary Fund and the Bank of England both said that the pound was overvalued prior to the 2016 vote, so you could argue that a dip *might* have been coming anyway.

The effect of Brexit on the housing market depends on who you talk to. In London and the south of England, Brexit uncertainty has had a dampening impact on house prices and overall confidence in the housing market — as does any major market uncertainty, of course — which, is resulting in fewer properties being put up for sale. But the effect outside of London and the south appears more limited. I would suggest that any effect is most likely short term and it's potentially a market ripe for investment as more savvy investors will be doing the opposite of the masses and investing now when there are great buying opportunities.

Chapter **4**

Everybody Needs Good Neighbors: Looking at Long-Term UK–EU Relations

I f you set foot in the United Kingdom (UK) at any point during the 1980s and 1990s, you'll be well familiar with the theme tune from *Neighbours*, the Australian soap opera that had Brits hooked when it first aired on the BBC in 1986. "Neighbors," the annoyingly catchy tune began, "everybody needs good neighbors. . . ." (The theme tune's still the same, by the way, even though the show was long ago relegated from the Beeb to Channel 5.)

And even though many Brits actively avoid making eye contact with their real-life neighbors, let alone bother to learn their names, the sentiment still means something. Everybody needs good neighbors, don't they?

And so I turn to the UK's neighbors on the continent, and the future (post-Brexit) relationship between the UK and the European Union (EU), as outlined in the joint political declaration released in November 2018.

Will "good neighbors become good friends," as the theme tune goes, or will there be passive-aggressive arguments over whose trash can is blocking whose driveway? Read on to find out.

Understanding the Declaration on Future Relations and How It Differs from the Withdrawal Agreement

November 2018 was a key point in the UK–EU negotiations, because the final draft withdrawal agreement (see Chapter 3) and political declaration on the future relationship were both released. Together, these documents gave everyone a much clearer idea of how Brexit — and life after Brexit — would play out. Most of the media attention focused on the withdrawal agreement, but the political declaration shouldn't be ignored.

The withdrawal agreement focuses on the exit process, but the *political declaration on future relations* (full title: "Political declaration setting out the framework for the future relationship between the European Union and the United Kingdom") looks beyond Brexit to outline how the two sides plan to work together in the future, after the end of any transition period (see Chapter 3).

REMEMBER

Unlike the withdrawal agreement, the political declaration on future relations (to save my fingers, I'm just going to call it "the declaration" from now on) isn't legally binding. Nor is it particularly detailed; the declaration is a trim 26 pages, compared to the whopping near-600 pages of the withdrawal deal.

If it's not legally binding, what's the point of the declaration? For one thing, it sets out a goal of continued close cooperation between the UK and the EU, establishing an "ambitious, broad, deep, and flexible partnership." In other words, the EU and the UK intend to remain friends.

REMEMBER

The declaration has also been described by the UK government as "a set of instructions to negotiators" who'll be sorting out the nitty-gritty aspects of the UK's ongoing relationship with the EU. In that way, it's like a stepping-stone on the road to negotiating a post-Brexit relationship.

Areas covered in the declaration include:

>> Trade

>> Economic cooperation

>> Law enforcement

>> Crime and justice

>> Security and defense

>> Foreign policy

REMEMBER

Formal negotiations on these areas won't begin until the UK exits the EU (whether that's in October 2019 or at a later date). In an ideal world, the two sides will agree as much as possible before the transition period ends in December 2020 (that's if the transition period isn't extended). But, in reality, the UK and EU are likely to be in negotiations for years to come.

And although both sides have said they want a relationship that's "as close as possible," until all post-Brexit negotiations have been completed, we don't know what that relationship will really look like in practice. That's why the declaration itself is pretty vague.

But let's look at what the agreement does say, and what this may mean for the UK. In this chapter, I largely focus on the parts of the declaration that will be of most interest to UK businesses.

Trading in Goods and Services in the Future

Although the UK no longer wants to be part of the EU, it certainly doesn't want to lose access to the world's largest single market, which is what the EU is. Likewise, the UK is an important customer for European goods and a critical partner in matters like security.

REMEMBER

Therefore, despite the political chatter and infighting, it's in the interests of both the UK and the EU to agree on a long-term trade arrangement that not only allows smooth trade between the two parties (thereby benefitting businesses and citizens on both sides) but also allows the two bodies to work together on areas like defense, security, fraud prevention, and so on.

Looking at the UK's potential trading relationship with the EU

The word *frictionless* is often mentioned in relation to future trade between the UK and the EU, but as the saying goes, there's no such thing as a free lunch. What I mean is, easy trade between the UK and the EU can only be achieved with a certain amount of regulatory compliance between the two.

REMEMBER

So, when the declaration states the intention of creating a trading relationship that's "as close as possible," it goes on to specify that "the Parties envisage comprehensive arrangements that will create a free-trade area, combining deep regulatory and customs cooperation, underpinned by provisions ensuring a level playing field for open and fair competition."

TECHNICAL STUFF

A *free-trade agreement* is an international trade agreement between two parties (usually between two countries, but in the case of the EU, the whole union negotiates with other countries as one trading bloc). Free-trade agreements are designed to boost international trade and make it easier for countries to trade. How? Mainly by cutting *tariffs* (taxes on imports and exports) and other trade barriers. Read more about how trade deals are negotiated in Chapter 5.

With the declaration wording as it is, the EU is subtly reminding the UK that the more economic rights it retains, the more EU obligations it'll need to sign on for. In other words, a free-trade agreement with the European single market will likely come at the price of accepting certain EU laws and product standards. That's the "level playing field" that the declaration is talking about.

Bottom line? "As close as possible" isn't the same as "frictionless," and you can expect trade to be one of the trickier factors in the UK's future negotiations with the EU.

TIP

At the time of writing, nothing has been agreed on UK–EU trade, and the vague "as close as possible" wording of the declaration opens up all sorts of potential trading scenarios. In Chapter 12, I speculate on some of these scenarios in more detail, and highlight other key Brexit developments to keep an eye on.

Considering whether the UK can just trade with the EU under World Trade Organization rules

The UK can certainly trade with the EU under World Trade Organization (WTO) rules. In fact, if the UK leaves the EU without getting parliamentary approval on the withdrawal deal (a "no-deal Brexit"; see Chapter 3), then WTO rules will immediately come into force (because no deal means no transition period).

REMEMBER

The WTO is the organization that helps countries negotiate the terms of international trade. When two trading partners (say, the UK and the EU) don't have a free-trade agreement in place, they trade under WTO rules. So, if the UK and the EU are unable to reach a trade agreement in the future, then they'll simply trade under WTO rules.

Trading under WTO rules would have its pluses and minuses for the UK. On the plus side:

>> With 164 members, the WTO covers 98 percent of global trade.

>> In the short term, WTO rules forbid the EU from imposing more checks on UK goods, while the UK abides by EU regulations.

But the downsides include the following:

>> No major country trades with the EU under WTO rules alone. Most choose to negotiate a separate free-trade agreement, or have additional agreements on top of the WTO rules. (The United States, for example, trades with the EU under WTO rules but has more than 20 additional agreements covering specific areas of trade.)

>> Tariffs can be pretty steep under WTO rules. For example, cars crossing the UK–EU border would be taxed at 10 percent.

REMEMBER

Overall, a specially negotiated free-trade agreement between the UK and the EU is likely to be more beneficial to both parties.

Seeing what will happen with trading in financial services

These days, the UK excels as a service-led country, particularly when it comes to financial services; the London financial sector is considered by many as the number-one financial market in the world. Billions of euros of European business loans are financed through London, so this is a key area of negotiations for both parties.

According to the declaration, the future agreement for financial services will be based on a system of "equivalence," which basically means London will need identical laws and regulations as EU financial sectors.

Both sides aim to have agreement on financial services sewn up by the end of June 2020. Whatever's agreed may potentially impact the overall UK economy because financial services — indeed, the services sector in general — form a key part of the UK economy.

Looking at UK trade with the rest of the world

As a member of the EU, the UK trades with countries around the world under preferential EU free-trade agreements — agreements that the UK will no longer be party to after Brexit (or, more specifically, after the end of any transition period).

This has prompted a mad rush to "roll over" as many of the existing beneficial trade agreements with non-EU countries as possible. However, as of February 2019, just one month before the original Brexit deadline of March 29, 2019, the UK government had only managed to roll over 7 of the 69 existing trade agreements. Those seven agreements were with Switzerland, Chile, Mauritius, Madagascar, Zimbabwe, the Faroe Islands, and the Seychelles.

That leaves a lot of agreements still to sort out with the UK's non-EU trading partners, including with major countries like Canada, Japan, and Turkey. And that's on top of negotiating the attractive new trade deals with countries like the United States, as promised during the referendum campaign.

REMEMBER

It's important to note that, under the terms of the withdrawal deal (see Chapter 3), the UK's pre-Brexit trading relationships with the rest of the world will still apply until the end of the transition period; after that, the UK will need to have its own trade agreements in place if it wants to retain the preferential access to worldwide markets that it has been used to. This will involve either rolling over existing trade agreements or negotiating whole new agreements.

Many of those in favor of Brexit are keen to point out the potentially huge opportunity the UK has to negotiate new free-trade deals with the rest of the world. Of course, the EU is a significant part of the worldwide economy, but it's dwarfed by the United States and China. And as emerging economies grow stronger, they may further tip the balance of economic power away from the world's largest single market.

REMEMBER

For example, a report by PricewaterhouseCoopers (PwC), titled *The World in 2050*, makes some interesting predictions about the global economic order in 2050, including the following:

>> Emerging markets could grow approximately twice as fast as advanced economies.

>> The EU27's share of global gross domestic product (GDP) will be 9 percent in 2050; China alone will account for 20 percent of global GDP.

REMEMBER

The *EU27* is the name given to the remaining 27 EU member states, excluding the UK.

>> The largest economies in the world are tipped to be China (first place), India (second place), the United States (third place), and Indonesia (fourth place).

>> The UK may drop down to tenth place, but remain above France and Italy.

>> The worldwide economy could double in size by 2050.

PwC's paper states that emerging economies will need to invest heavily in infrastructure if they're going to realize their growth potential. This need for emerging economies to invest in infrastructure could lead to significant business opportunities for the UK (and the EU, for that matter).

Building Regulatory Cooperation between the UK and the EU

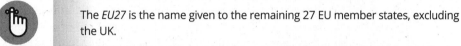

Central to all future trade talks between the UK and the EU is this idea of a level playing field, meaning similar or identical rules and regulations on either side. So, although the declaration talks about the "regulatory autonomy" of both sides, it also talks about "common principles in the fields of standardization, technical regulations, conformity assessment, accreditation, market surveillance, metrology, and labeling."

REMEMBER

The declaration also talks about the level playing field in terms of "state aid, competition, social and employment standards, environmental standards, climate change, and relevant tax matters." So, from a practical point of view, this may mean the UK has to align with the EU on matters like value-added tax (VAT) rates, state assistance, and employment law.

Remember that, as a non-EU country, the UK will have no say whatsoever in how these rules and regulations are decided. This has plenty of people worried that the UK will simply have to follow where the EU leads (in terms of rules), with no role in shaping those rules.

WARNING

Employment law is a particularly interesting area to watch because the UK's two main political parties have quite different stances in this area. The Labour Party has been very vocal in relation to future protections for employees, while the Conservative government has, over the last few years, attempted to weaken employee rights (for instance, by giving employers an extended period under which they can make new staff redundant with no reason).

Alignment with the EU may not just affect the UK's own laws and practices; it may also limit the UK's ability to strike trade deals with non-EU countries. For example, the UK may be prevented from accepting certain goods from non-EU countries that don't meet EU standards. Or, if the UK joins a customs union with the EU, as many in the UK Parliament have proposed, it'll mean the UK charging the same external tariffs as the EU — another factor that may limit the UK's ability to strike new trade deals.

Solving the Thorny Issue of Customs Arrangements

Closely related to trade and regulatory alignment is the issue of customs arrangements.

Aiming for tariff-free trade with Europe

Here's what the declaration has to say about customs:

> The economic partnership should ensure no tariffs, fees, charges, or quantitative restrictions across all sectors, with ambitious customs arrangements that, in line with the Parties' objectives and principles above, build and improve on the single customs territory provided for in the Withdrawal Agreement. . . .

Sounds good right, no tariffs or other customs barriers to trade? Yet customs arrangements are likely to be a major bone of contention between the UK and the EU.

REMEMBER

For one thing, many are concerned that the temporary customs arrangements set out in the withdrawal agreement (see Chapter 3), particularly in relation to Northern Ireland, will end up tying the UK to some sort of permanent customs union. The declaration wording does little to allay those specific fears, except to say that both sides are open to any permanent solution that avoids a hard Irish border and indefinite backstop.

If the UK were tied to the European customs union indefinitely, it might restrict the UK's ability to strike independent trade deals with other countries, and mean the UK has to continue to follow EU rules and regulations.

Those on the UK side might prefer to create a new single customs territory with the EU, which would allow the UK free access to the EU market, without compromising the integrity of the EU's single market. But, at the time of writing, we don't yet know what the formal customs arrangements will be and how they may restrict the UK's ability to strike trade deals with other trading partners around the world.

Knowing what will happen to VAT on goods from the EU

Under EU rules, VAT is not payable on goods imported from within the EU. Depending on the customs arrangement agreed between the UK and the EU, this may well change, and UK businesses may need to change their VAT processes.

For example, if the UK were to revert to WTO rules for trade with the EU, then VAT would be payable upon the arrival of those goods within the UK. This would create a cash-flow nightmare for many businesses in the UK, and it has prompted the government to promise that it will step in to help businesses overcome this potential VAT nightmare.

WARNING

I talk more about VAT and importing and exporting in Chapter 5, but remember that VAT is an extremely technical topic. Always talk to your accountant about VAT rules and have her clarify any changes you need to make to your VAT processes.

Considering What "No More Free Movement" Will Mean in Practice

A key promise of Brexit was that the UK would take back control of its borders and stop the free movement of people from the EU. This is confirmed in both the withdrawal deal and the declaration. In theory, this position won't change; however, if the UK decided to remain in the EU single market after Brexit (see Chapter 1), then it would have no choice but to accept free movement of people. This prospect seems unlikely, though, and, at the time of writing, the intention is for free movement to end after Brexit.

REMEMBER

With this in mind, the declaration recognizes that "the principle of free movement of persons between the Union and the United Kingdom will no longer apply" after the transition period has ended. The flip side, of course, is that Brits will no longer be freely able to live, work, study, or retire in the EU.

But don't worry, this won't affect your summer holiday to Tuscany or Corfu. The declaration says that both sides aim to allow "visa-free travel" for short-term visits. Longer-term stays and employment, on the other hand, may require a visa — although, like everything else in the declaration, this is yet to be negotiated in any detail.

Depending on what the UK agrees with the EU, after the end of the transition period, EU citizens who want to come and work in the UK may have to apply for a skilled worker visa. They may also have to meet minimum salary requirements if the UK government's proposed immigration plans come into force (see Chapter 3). Low-skilled workers from the EU, who are so vital for sectors like agriculture, will likely be allowed to work in the UK for up to 12 months without needing a visa.

REMEMBER

The declaration also states that the UK will have to treat citizens of all EU member states in the same way — so, the UK can't, for example, allow workers from Spain to come to the UK without a visa while insisting on visas for workers from Bulgaria and Romania. (Ireland will be the only exception to this rule because the UK and Ireland already have a separate arrangement for free movement between the two; Ireland will be treated differently from other EU member states, and that's fine.)

Read more about the UK government's immigration plans in Chapter 3 and employing EU citizens in Chapter 7.

Forming the Basis for Formal Post-Brexit Negotiations

Remember that the declaration isn't legally binding, which means everything contained in it is still, at the time of writing, up for negotiation — including whether the UK will enter into a permanent customs union with the EU, as many in the UK Parliament are pushing for (see Chapter 3).

REMEMBER

Things like trade and economic cooperation can't be officially negotiated until the UK finally leaves the EU, but the declaration itself could potentially be amended before the exit date. For example, if the UK Parliament reached a consensus on joining a customs union with the EU, then the declaration may need to be amended to reflect that before the withdrawal agreement can be approved by Parliament.

But assuming the declaration stays as it is for now, how will it underpin ongoing UK–EU negotiations? Read on.

Preparing for a potentially bumpy road ahead

What will these ongoing negotiations look like? Well, if you thought the withdrawal agreement and political declaration were difficult to negotiate, you ain't seen nothing yet! Negotiating every aspect of the UK's ongoing relationship with the EU will probably take years and will no doubt prompt some juicy insults and burns on both sides, just as the withdrawal negotiations did. (See Chapter 3 for some of the best quotes to come out of the withdrawal negotiations.)

The declaration may state the intention of remaining "as close as possible," but you know what they say about good intentions and the road to hell. Glass-half-empty types may point out that we don't yet know how those good intentions will hold up under the strains of tough negotiations, where each side is out to protect its own interests.

As a glass-half-full type, I prefer to put a more positive spin on the negotiations. It may not always be obvious, but there's a general consensus between the UK and the EU to find workable solutions while maintaining their independence and negotiating positions. It's in both sides' interests to find common ground.

Looking at some of the factors that may impact negotiations and future relations

Considering that the negotiations are likely to take a while, what sort of issues are there on the horizon that may influence (and/or be influenced by) negotiations? Let's take a look:

>> If there's a change in UK government or prime minister, will that bring a totally different approach to the post-Brexit negotiations? Probably, especially if Theresa May were to be replaced with a hardline Brexiteer prime minister. The next general election is scheduled for May 2022, although the Labour Party has called for an earlier election (and Theresa May isn't averse to calling snap elections herself).

>> Scotland will leave the EU with the rest of the UK, despite the people of Scotland voting firmly in favor of remaining in the EU. Will Scotland hold a new independence referendum and decide to leave the UK? If so, will that impact the UK's negotiating position?

>> Will a rise in nationalism across the EU dilute the current move toward a federal Europe? If so, will this weaken the EU's negotiating position?

>> How will the EU Parliament elections in May 2019 impact the shape and timing of ongoing UK–EU relations? At the time of writing, the UK was reluctantly

preparing to take part in EU elections and select its own Members of the European Parliament (MEPs) — even though those MEPs may only be in their posts for a few months, if the UK leaves the EU in October 2019, as planned.

In Chapter 12, you can find ten other Brexit developments to keep an eye on.

AND NOW FOR THE REALLY IMPORTANT QUESTIONS: CAN THE UK STILL TAKE PART IN EUROVISION AND THE EUROPEAN CHAMPIONSHIP?

Brits have a love–hate relationship with the Eurovision Song Contest — or, rather, they absolutely love to hate it. If they're honest, they get a kick out of the silly songs, the daft costumes, the nonsensical lyrics, and the obviously pre-arranged voting patterns. Hours of bureaucracy, broken up by terrible music? You had them at "hours"!

That's why, every year, Brits show up and take their annual beating with as much pride as anyone taking part in Eurovision can muster.

You'll be pleased to know that Brexit won't change this. Not one silly little bit. As a member of the European Broadcasting Union (EBU), the UK will still be allowed to participate in Eurovision. The EBU is totally separate from the EU, and when you keep in mind that Israel and Australia already take part in the contest, it's clear that the "Euro" in "Eurovision" is used in the loosest possible sense. By this point, it looks like Eurovision will take anyone who can be bothered to show up, regardless of their geographical location.

And what about the UEFA European Football Championship? Surely they won't kick UK teams out of Euro 2020? (When it comes to international football, the UK nations of England, Scotland, Wales, and Northern Ireland compete separately.) For England fans, in particular, not competing in the Euros is unthinkable — especially now that England has pulled together the best team in years and finally has a manager who's (for now, at least) universally loved.

Again, Brexit won't change the UK teams' roles in the European Championship. As members of the Union of European Football Associations (UEFA), the English, Northern Irish, Scottish, and Welsh football teams will still be able to participate in the Euros. ***Remember:*** The likes of Switzerland and Russia are not in the EU but still take part.

So, rest easy, readers, knowing that the UK's participation in the sequins and silliness of Eurovision, and the goals and gaffs of European football, will continue for many years.

3

Getting Down to Business: The Impact of Brexit on UK Companies

Prepare for changes in importing and exporting to and from the European Union.

Look at potential transport and logistics hurdles that may result from Brexit.

Understand employment issues.

Get ready for other potential business impacts of Brexit.

Undertake a Brexit impact assessment for your business.

Chapter **5**

Importing and Exporting Goods and Services between the UK and the EU

B ack in the oh-so-innocent days of July 2017 — at a time when the United Kingdom (UK) had barely begun formal negotiations with the European Union (EU) on a Brexit withdrawal agreement — the UK's international trade secretary, Liam Fox, gave an interview to BBC Radio 4's *Today* program. In that interview, he uttered the words, "The free trade agreement that we will have to do with the European Union should be one of the easiest in human history."

One of the easiest in human history. Let that prediction sink in for a moment. Given that the UK–EU negotiations on the withdrawal agreement were anything but easy (and remembering that the withdrawal agreement only covers the UK's *exit* from the EU, not its long-term trading relationship — see Chapter 3), Fox's words seem a little too . . . optimistic.

Given that the UK Parliament didn't even agree on what sort of Brexit it wanted, Fox's words are bordering on delusional. (To borrow a sentiment from *When Harry Met Sally . . .*, "I'll have what he's having!") As we well know, nothing about Brexit is easy.

In reality, agreeing on a trade deal is likely to be a lengthy, complicated process, and we don't yet know the full implications of any such trade deal for British (and European) businesses. Therefore, in this chapter, I lay out where things stand for now, and look at how things may pan out in the short and long term for UK businesses that import or export.

Looking at UK Trade around the World

Naturally, most of this chapter focuses on importing and exporting between the UK and the EU. But before I get to that subject, I thought it might be helpful to put UK–EU trade in context of the broader UK trading picture.

According to figures from the Office for National Statistics (ONS):

>> In the calendar year 2018, total UK trade (with the entire world), amounted to £1,291 billion (up 2.5 percent from the previous year).

>> Of that £1,291 billion, imports totaled £661.7 billion (up 3.1 percent) and exports totaled £629.4 billion (up 1.9 percent).

>> Goods accounted for £838.8 billion (up 3 percent), while services accounted for £452.3 billion (up 1.7 percent).

As for the split between the EU and rest of the world, according to 2017 ONS figures, UK–EU trade accounted for £619.3 billion (up 11.5 percent), while UK trade with non-EU countries totaled £639.8 billion (up 8.6 percent).

REMEMBER

In other words, trade between the UK and the EU makes up a little under half of all UK trade. However, trade between the UK and non-EU countries is growing at a faster pace, indicating that non-EU trade is likely to become a bigger piece of the pie as emerging economies grow stronger. These figures also don't reflect that some goods from the UK pass through European ports like Rotterdam before being shipped elsewhere in the world.

Who are the UK's biggest trading partners? According to the ONS, the UK's top ten trading partners during 2017 were:

1. **United States:** £183.2 billion
2. **Germany:** £134.9 billion
3. **Netherlands:** £85.7 billion
4. **France:** £81.4 billion
5. **China:** £67 billion
6. **Ireland:** £58.7 billion
7. **Spain:** £48.6 billion
8. **Belgium:** £47.1 billion
9. **Italy:** £43.1 billion
10. **Switzerland:** £32.1 billion

A lot of European countries are on that list! However, it's important to note that the UK has a trade surplus with the United States. That means the UK currently exports more to the U.S. than it imports, making the United States a key market for UK businesses. The UK also has a trade surplus with Ireland and Switzerland, while it has trade deficits (meaning the UK imports more than it exports) with Germany, the Netherlands, China, Spain, Belgium, and Italy. The UK has a balanced trade account with France.

HOW DO TRADE AGREEMENTS WORK?

Countries agree on trade deals with each other to make trade easier and cheaper, thereby encouraging increased international trade.

There are a few different types of international trade agreements, but by far the most common types are *free-trade agreements,* which is the kind the UK hopes to agree on with the EU, or *preferential-trade agreements.*

A free-trade agreement stipulates tariff-free trade — or, sometimes, reduced tariffs — on all goods moving between the parties. Free-trade agreements may also stipulate other conditions, such as free movement of people and money, investment guarantees, or requirements for both parties to uphold certain standards and regulations. Meanwhile, a preferential-trade agreement is much less broad and is designed to reduce (not abolish) tariffs, and usually on certain products only, rather than all products.

(continued)

(continued)

Trade agreements are typically *bilateral* (signed by two parties, such as the EU and the UK) or *multilateral* (signed by three or more parties, usually neighboring countries — the North American Free Trade Agreement [NAFTA] is one example of this approach).

The EU negotiates trade agreements together as one big bloc. So, the UK can't, for example, make one free-trade agreement with France and another free-trade agreement with Germany.

A free-trade agreement of the type the UK would ideally like to agree on with the EU looks to encourage trade by eliminating or reducing *trade barriers* (any government measure that restricts or impedes trade between countries). Common examples of trade barriers include:

- **Quotas:** A physical limit on the quantity of certain goods that can be imported into a country, usually done to protect domestic producers

- **Tariffs:** Effectively, a tax or financial penalty on imported goods

- **Customs duties:** A tax applied on imported goods

The terms *tariff* and *customs duty* are often used interchangeably because both basically mean a tax applied by the government on imported goods (very rarely, exported goods). Technically speaking, *tariff* refers to the overall framework for taxing imported goods, while *customs duty* refers to the specific income that the government collects as a result of the tariff.

For example, let's say the UK government decides to impose a 12 percent tariff on imports of men's underpants. As a result of this tariff, the customs duty on a pair of £5 underpants would be 60 pence. The tariff is the tax set by the government, while the duty is the actual income the government receives.

Having said that, I'm sure no one will throw a hissy fit if you use the terms tariff and *customs duty* interchangeably. Most people do!

Understanding Big-Picture Importing and Exporting Issues

On a very broad scale, what does Brexit mean for UK imports and exports?

Negotiating future trading relationships

After the UK leaves the EU, their future trading relationship will depend on what sort of trade agreement the UK strikes with the EU. (See the sidebar "How do trade agreements work?")

That's if the UK manages to strike a trade deal with the EU at all — given how the withdrawal negotiations have progressed, and the fact that everyone has different ideas on the UK's ideal relationship with Europe, you probably shouldn't take it for granted that there'll ever be a formal free-trade agreement between the UK and the EU.

REMEMBER

Negotiating a free-trade agreement takes time — a lot of time. For example, the EU began trade talks with Japan in 2013. An agreement was finally approved at the end of 2018, and it came into force in February 2019. That's pretty much normal for a big trade deal like the EU–Japan deal. So, it's likely to be a while before UK businesses have any long-term certainty on what happens with their EU imports and exports.

After the UK leaves the EU, the UK will begin negotiating a trade agreement with the EU — while also negotiating new trade deals with other trading partners around the world. This is necessary because the UK will no longer be covered by EU trade agreements with countries around the world, so the UK will have to renegotiate or "roll over" existing trade deals with its non-EU partners, if it wants to continue trading on preferential terms.

The impact of deal or no deal

If the UK manages to agree on some sort of withdrawal deal with the EU (whether it's Theresa May's deal, as outlined in Chapter 3, or another, freshly negotiated withdrawal deal), then UK–EU trade will continue as normal for the duration of any agreed-upon transition period. The idea is that both parties will start to negotiate a longer-term trade agreement during that transition period.

If no new trade deal is negotiated during the transition period, then the UK will trade with the EU under World Trade Organization (WTO) rules until a trade deal is agreed upon. (See Chapter 4 for more on how the WTO works.)

Likewise, if the UK exits the EU without securing a withdrawal agreement, and without any form of transition period, then WTO rules would come into force right away. Many people have portrayed trading under WTO rules as a worst-case scenario, but WTO provides a baseline for trade between countries. Trading under WTO rules would work, but it wouldn't be as advantageous as a specially negotiated free-trade deal (or EU membership).

Whatever happens with the UK's exit from the EU, trade won't grind to a halt while new deals are being negotiated or in the unlikely event of a no-deal Brexit. But trade may be subject to more stringent customs rules and tariffs.

Stripping back the hype on tariffs

Tariffs (see the sidebar "How do trade agreements work?") increase the costs of importing and exporting goods. Yet, in my opinion, we're unlikely to see very steep tariffs being applied.

I find it helpful to consider the subject of tariffs within the wider context of currency exchange rates. The currently weaker pound makes British goods cheaper for overseas customers, which is advantageous for UK companies that export. So, if, for example, the EU applied a 5 percent tariff on British cars being sold in Europe, yes, that makes British cars more expensive for European customers, but that's offset by the weaker pound.

The fact that the UK refused to adopt the euro puts UK businesses in a very different position from their EU counterparts, with the ability to benefit from currency swings (compared to, say, a German company trading with a French company, where both are operating within the eurozone).

The *eurozone* is the name given to EU member countries that have adopted the euro currency. Read more EU-related jargon and definitions in Chapter 1.

UK businesses are already used to coping with exchange rate swings between the pound and the euro. If they also have to cope with new tariffs, will that send companies bust? Probably not, at least not in profitable, well-run businesses that are operating on healthy margins. (The trouble, of course, comes for businesses who are operating on very tight margins. Also, importers, who already see their costs rise when the pound is weak, may struggle more with the introduction of tariffs.)

In response to concerns about tariffs in the event of a no-deal Brexit, in March 2019, the UK government set out its plan to temporarily slash tariffs on non-EU imports while introducing tariffs on EU imports. This was designed to encourage more non-EU trade, while giving a symbolic middle finger to the EU (something that various UK governments have enjoyed doing as often as possible for decades).

How helpful this would be in reality remains to be seen. (Would a business realistically switch from importing goods from Italy to importing goods from, say, Zimbabwe overnight to avoid paying customs duties? Not likely.) It's also unclear whether the UK would even be able to introduce tariffs on EU goods under WTO rules, while there is parity between EU and UK laws (parity on laws usually prevents countries from penalizing one another with tariffs, according to the WTO). And, if the UK did introduce tariffs on EU goods, would the EU respond with equal (or potentially higher) tariffs on UK goods? Probably. So many unknowns, so little time. . . .

I don't mean to downplay the impact of tariffs on businesses. Instead, I think it's important to keep the issue of tariffs in perspective.

TIP

Whether it's Brexit or any other dramatic market event, the key to riding out business uncertainty or market fluctuations is making sure your business is as efficient and profitable as possible. If you have concerns about the impact of tariffs on your business, consider working with a business adviser to find ways to increase your profitability and reduce business costs.

Will UK Businesses Lose Access to the Single Market?

In a word, no. British businesses won't lose access to EU countries as a result of Brexit. Read on to find out why.

Whatever happens, trade will continue

If the UK government is able to pass a withdrawal agreement, then, when the UK leaves the EU, it would enter a transition period. Under May's withdrawal deal, this transition period would last until the end of December 2020, and could potentially be extended until 2022.

During the course of any transition period, trading terms between the UK and EU would remain the same, meaning frictionless movement of goods with no tariffs. Both sides would use this transition period to start negotiations on a formal trade agreement, ideally a free-trade agreement (see the sidebar "How do trade agreements work?").

However, if the UK leaves the EU without approving a withdrawal agreement (known as *no-deal Brexit*), then there would be no transitional period, and trade between the UK and EU would be covered by WTO rules, until a new trade agreement is reached. The UK and the EU are both members of the WTO, which allows them to trade under WTO rules until a free-trade agreement is negotiated.

Some people have suggested that if the UK failed to approve a withdrawal deal, the EU would play "hardball" and impose tough tariffs to penalize the UK government. But that looks like scaremongering. (In fact, it's the UK government that's been threatening sanctions on EU goods.) Under WTO rules, countries are not allowed to discriminate against trading partners where their regulations are in tandem.

REMEMBER

Under either scenario (withdrawal deal with transition period or no-deal Brexit and WTO rules), trade between the UK and the EU will continue.

The importance of EU markets to UK businesses

With the EU accounting for more than half of the UK's international trade, there's no doubt that Europe is a key market for British businesses.

Europe is geographically close, it's relatively easy to transport goods to and from, and it's culturally close to the UK in terms of the goods consumed. Therefore, access to the EU single market (see Chapter 1) is vital for UK businesses.

REMEMBER

Any suggestions that UK exporters would be "cut off" from trading with European customers after Brexit is pure hysteria. British companies won't be barred from trading with their European counterparts.

It's true that tariffs may come into play (depending on what's agreed between the UK and the EU), and that importing and exporting to and from Europe may become more complicated, especially in the unlikely event of a no-deal Brexit (see the section "Planning for Changes in UK–EU Imports and Exports"). There may be challenges, additional costs, time delays and no doubt political friction, but the UK could not be "frozen out" of EU markets — and vice versa.

The importance of the UK market to EU businesses

Many of the biggest players in Europe have a trade surplus with the UK. Germany, Spain, Italy, Belgium, the Netherlands — all of these countries export more to the UK than they import from the UK. In other words, it's in Europe's interests for UK–EU trade to continue as smoothly as possible after Brexit, just as it's in the interests of the UK.

In February 2019, German newspaper *Welt am Sonntag* reported that Germany would be hard hit if the UK crashed out of the EU without securing a withdrawal agreement (thereby immediately forcing the UK and EU to trade under WTO rules instead of having a softer transition period).

The paper cited a joint study by the Halle Institute for Economic Research and the Martin Luther University of Halle-Wittenberg, which found that as many as 100,000 German jobs could be threatened by a hard, no-deal Brexit. Workers in the German car industry would likely take the biggest hit.

The Republic of Ireland would also be hit hard if trade between the UK and the EU became more difficult. At the time of writing, Ireland exports around 250,000 tons of beef a year into the UK — that's almost half of all Irish beef production.

REMEMBER

Bottom line? Both sides will benefit from a trading relationship that's as smooth as possible. Both sides will suffer if that's not achieved. During future trade negotiations, it's vital that the two parties work to agree on a mutually beneficial agreement, giving access to each other's markets in a way that's as seamless as possible. Turn back to Chapter 4 to read more about future negotiations between the UK and the EU.

Planning for Changes in UK–EU Imports and Exports

Until we know under what sort of withdrawal terms the UK will exit the EU, and until we know how the longer-term trade negotiations shake out between the two parties, there's little certainty for companies that import or export to and from the EU. But this section covers what we *do* know. . . .

Factoring in potential new tariffs

The UK government is looking for tariff-free access to the EU single market, coupled with complete freedom to negotiate free-trade deals with other countries around the world. (As the saying goes, we want to "have our cake and eat it, too!")

But this won't be an easy thing to secure (turn back to Chapter 4 to read about the complexities surrounding the UK and EU's future relationship). Anyone who implies otherwise is either deliberately telling fibs or is unaware of the massive complexities involved in negotiating trade agreements.

REMEMBER

Tariff-free trade comes at other costs, such as free movement of people, a customs union, identical (or very similar) rules and regulations, and so on. In particular, the EU is unlikely to compromise on the regulations and safety aspects associated with the single market.

Let's take the commonly quoted examples of chlorinated chicken from the United States and hormone-treated beef from Australia, both of which are outlawed under EU laws. At the time of writing, UK laws are effectively the same as EU laws when it comes to food health and safety. So, after Brexit, if the UK changed its food standards to allow the import of chlorinated chicken from the United States and hormone-treated beef from Australia, this would go against current EU regulations — potentially limiting the UK's ability to strike a free-trade deal with the EU. In theory, it's possible that the UK could agree on a dual system of regulation with the EU, but it seems unlikely.

Therefore, although the UK's starting point is tariff-free trade with Europe, that may not be where we end up. If tariffs are introduced (either as a result of a no-deal Brexit and WTO rules, or as part of a future trade agreement), this will make British products more expensive to EU customers and EU imports more expensive for British businesses. Businesses will need to prepare for this eventuality and maximize their margins wherever possible.

TIP

The following government resources will help you keep abreast of tariff developments:

>> www.gov.uk/trade-tariff: This website is a general starting point.

>> www.trade-tariff.service.gov.uk/trade-tariff/sections: Here you can look up tariff rates by product category.

>> www.gov.uk/guidance/check-temporary-rates-of-customs-duty-on-imports-after-eu-exit: Here you can find advice on the temporary tariff regime that will apply in the event of a no-deal Brexit.

Coping with more paperwork and higher costs

Regardless of whether the UK and the EU agree on a withdrawal deal and then a trade arrangement, there may still be an increase in import and export paperwork and costs for UK and European companies.

WARNING

Work closely with your accountant to monitor your costs and cash flow extremely carefully in the aftermath of Brexit.

The impact will be significantly greater in the event of a no-deal Brexit because UK companies importing and exporting goods to and from the EU would require:

>> Export declarations

>> Import declarations

>> Safety and security declarations

>> UK import/export license

>> UK economic operator registration and identification (EORI) number

They would also need to:

>> Include international terms and conditions of service in contracts with EU customers

>> Consider engaging a customs broker to look after software and Her Majesty's Revenue & Customs (HMRC) authorizations (read more about value-added tax [VAT] in the next section)

>> Ensure the correct classification and value of goods

>> Pay VAT and import duties unless the goods are entered into "duty suspension" via an authorized customs warehouse, or postponed accounting rules come into play (again, more on that next)

In the event of a no-deal Brexit, there have been suggestions that the potential £39 billion saved by not paying the "divorce bill" (see Chapter 3) could be used to help UK companies cope with these higher costs. However, people have also proposed lots of other uses for that money, including more funding for the National Health Service (NHS). Not paying the divorce bill isn't a "magic bullet" to solve any and all Brexit-related costs. Besides, the EU has said it would expect the divorce bill to be paid before it enters into trade negotiations with the UK.

And what if the UK exits *with* a withdrawal deal (whether it's Theresa May's agreement or an alternative arrangement)? In the short term, importing and exporting will continue as normal for the duration of the agreed-upon transition period. But after the transition period ends, importing and exporting paperwork will depend on what sort of trade agreement the UK and EU come up with. Much of the same paperwork listed earlier may still be required. For now, it's a case of "watch this space." (Turn to Chapter 12 to read about more Brexit "uncertainties" to keep an eye on.)

Remember that, after Brexit, goods moving between the UK and the EU may be subject to stricter customs checks and potential customs delays. Read more about these logistical challenges in Chapter 6.

Understanding the impact on import VAT and customs duties

We know that Brexit is likely to impact customs duties (see the sidebar "How do trade agreements work?") and import VAT.

TECHNICAL STUFF

Here's the difference between import VAT and customs and excise duties:

>> **Import VAT** is a tax applied by the government on goods that come into the country from other countries. Import VAT is charged at a set rate, which is currently 20 percent in the UK.

>> **Customs duty** is another tax applied by the government on goods imported from other countries. Different rates apply to different categories of products.

>> In the UK, **excise duty** is applied to alcoholic drinks, tobacco, and oil products (including petrol), regardless of whether the goods were produced in the UK. Different rates apply to different categories of goods.

Although the UK is a member of the EU, customs duties don't apply on goods arriving from the EU. Likewise, import VAT is effectively suspended on goods arriving from the EU, meaning you don't have to cough up for import VAT as soon as the goods arrive in the UK. Instead, you charge your end customer VAT and roll that VAT in with your annual VAT return.

After the UK leaves the EU, however, things get more complicated, particularly in the event of a no-deal Brexit. In the following sections, I walk you through the different scenarios.

No-deal Brexit: The UK leaves with no withdrawal agreement

Broadly speaking, goods being traded between the UK and the EU would be subject to the same rules as non-EU countries, which means customs and excise duties will apply immediately. Also, import VAT would technically be payable right away when the goods arrive in the UK, which would plunge many companies into a cash-flow nightmare. The government has, therefore, pledged to help businesses by implementing "postponed accounting," which means VAT on imported goods can be accounted for in the annual tax return instead of paying it as soon as the goods arrive in the UK.

Customs warehouses can be used to delay tax liability on imports. These warehouses are authorized by HMRC to store goods and suspend customs duty and import VAT until the goods leave the warehouse. Visit www.gov.uk/government/ publications/notice-3001-special-procedures-for-the-union-customs-code/annex-a to read more about customs warehouses.

REMEMBER

Always check the latest government advice on customs and excise duty and import VAT in the event of a no-deal Brexit. Head to www.gov.uk/government/ publications/partnership-pack-preparing-for-a-no-deal-eu-exit/ changes-to-customs-excise-and-vat-you-need-to-know-about-if-there-is-no-deal for the latest advice.

The UK leaves with an approved withdrawal agreement

Under this scenario, in the short term at least, nothing will change. Customs duty will not be payable on goods moving between the UK and the EU for the duration of the transition period. Likewise, VAT would continue to be suspended. What happens after the end of the transition period will depend on what's agreed upon during trade negotiations.

Ultimately, even if the UK exits the EU with a withdrawal deal and negotiates a trade agreement with the EU, the rules for customs duties and VAT on imported goods may change. One thing's for sure: The closer the UK's future trade relationship with the EU, the easier it'll be to manage VAT.

WARNING

VAT is an extremely complex subject. Always work with an accountant to clarify your VAT obligations and ensure your VAT procedures are correct.

And What About Services?

The UK is a service-oriented country. One commonly quoted statistic is that services make up 80 percent of the UK's economy. What's more, according to a study by the Tony Blair Institute for Global Change, services have driven three-fifths of the increase in UK exports over the last 20 years. If it weren't for Brexit-related disruption, the study claims exports of UK services would've outstripped goods exports within five years.

So, why has this chapter talked mainly about importing and exporting goods rather than services? It's because services trade agreements are notoriously complicated to negotiate.

Tariffs don't apply on services. Instead, negotiating the trading of services tends to rely on close regulatory compliance between the two parties. So, as part of negotiating a UK–EU free-trade agreement, both parties will have to negotiate regulations and requirements for services on a *sector-by-sector* basis. This is, to put it politely, extremely ambitious.

The truth is, there's no one-size-fits-all approach for trade agreements when it comes to services; some trade agreements barely cover services at all, while others only cover certain sectors. The recent EU–Canada trade deal, for instance, doesn't allow Canadian financial services companies to sell their services in the EU.

So, the ability of UK service companies to easily do business in the EU will depend on what the two parties agree on as part of the trade negotiations.

Critical to the smooth trading of services between the UK and EU is the notion of *passporting*, which allows UK firms to do business in the EU without having to gain authorization from each relevant member state. In other words, it allows UK companies to trade in the EU with much less red tape. If the UK leaves the EU in an orderly way, with a withdrawal agreement and transition period, these passporting rights will continue to apply in the short term.

However, if the UK leaves with no deal and is subject to WTO rules, then services businesses may be hit hard. That's because WTO rules barely touch on services. If the UK ends up trading with the EU under WTO rules, then the UK financial sector, for example, could, in theory, lose its passporting rights and would have to secure authorization to do business in European countries.

Going Further Afield: Trading With Customers outside of the EU

As head of the Commonwealth, in theory the UK has access to all Commonwealth trading markets. The population of the Commonwealth is 2.4 billion (EU population: 512 million), and 60 percent of the Commonwealth population are 29 years of age or under — which has led many commentators to point to the Commonwealth as a great opportunity for UK exporters. In addition, in 2017, the combined value of Commonwealth economies was $10.4 trillion and this is expected to increase to $13 trillion in 2020 (not to be sneezed at when you consider that the UK economy is valued at around $2.8 trillion).

India has the largest population in the Commonwealth, at around 1.2 billion people, so this potentially represents a significant market for UK businesses. However, India is a notoriously tough cookie when it comes to negotiating trade agreements.

In fact, when the EU and India tried to agree on a trade deal, talks stalled thanks to the UK's objections. For one thing, the UK objected to Indian tariffs on Scotch whisky. But, even more important, the UK had serious reservations about India's request for much freer movement between India and the EU as part of a trade deal. Given that the UK has been keen to cut migration from Europe, the chances of implementing a more liberal visa scheme for Indian citizens seems fairly unlikely. So, whether the UK will be able to agree on a trade deal with India remains to be seen. One thing is clear: The EU is keen as mustard to restart talks with India after the UK leaves the EU. With the UK out of the picture, an EU–India trade deal may progress much more smoothly.

This points to a wider issue in negotiating trade deals. Namely, are we likely to see more countries pushing for greater access to the UK job market in return for a trade deal? And, if so, is the UK likely to bend to such demands? (After all, many people point out that negotiating as part of a bloc, which is what the UK did as a member of the EU, affords much more negotiating power than negotiating as a standalone country.) And how would such a move go down with British voters, a large number of whom voted to end free movement from Europe?

Read more about the UK's trade negotiations with the rest of the world in Chapter 4.

IN THIS CHAPTER

» **Scoping out the big-picture issues around transport and logistics**

» **Dealing with changes to border controls**

» **Having the right paperwork for vehicles travelling in Europe**

» **Preparing the business for supply chain disruption**

» **Transporting goods to and from non-EU countries**

Chapter **6**

Tackling Transport and Logistics Challenges

Most industries will be touched by Brexit in one way or another, but some are bracing for a much greater impact. The United Kingdom (UK) transport and logistics industry is one such industry that faces significant challenges as a result of Brexit.

From big-picture issues like restricted access to qualified drivers, to nitty-gritty questions like "What happens when our delivery trucks reach the European Union (EU) border?," businesses operating in the UK transport and logistics industry face an uncertain time.

REMEMBER

Even if you don't run a logistics company, your business may still be affected by these issues. If you send goods to customers, for instance, even just within the UK, you may be hit by unexpected delays or higher costs. Or you may see your warehousing costs rise as other businesses look to stockpile goods amidst uncertainty, putting pressure on warehouse availability.

DRIVING THE FAMILY CAR IN EUROPE AFTER BREXIT

Let's say you drive to France every summer for your family vacation. Or maybe you pop over to Bruges every December in the car to stock up on Belgian beer and chocolate for Christmas presents. What hoops will British drivers have to jump through for personal travel in Europe?

First, after Brexit, you may still be affected by delays at ports, so always check the latest travel updates before you set off.

You may also need to carry additional documentation with you. That's because, although the UK is a member of the EU, UK drivers are entitled to drive in the EU using their UK driving licenses. That's likely to change after Brexit.

In the unlikely event of a no-deal Brexit:

- **You'll need to buy an International Driving Permit (IDP) to drive in EU countries (except Ireland, where the IDP isn't necessary for UK drivers).** IDPs are issued by the Post Office, and the type of IDP you need depends on which country or countries you're planning on driving in. Read more about IDPs at www.gov.uk/driving-abroad/international-driving-permit. Bear in mind that you'll still need to carry your driver's license with you when driving in Europe; the IDP doesn't replace the license.

- **The insurance industry is advising British motorists to get a Green Card from their car insurance providers.** This will prove that you have third-party insurance coverage in Europe.

- **You should display a GB sticker on the back of your car.**

And if the UK does leave under the terms of a withdrawal deal, meaning the UK enters a transition period? In theory, British drivers would be treated the same as European drivers for the duration of the transition period, which means no need for an IDP, Green Card, or GB sticker — for now.

My advice? Play it safe and cough up for the IDP (which, at the time of writing, costs only £5.50 per permit), get a GB sticker, and talk to your insurance provider about getting a Green Card.

In the UK, the RAC and AA provide lots of helpful, up-to-date advice for motorists driving in the EU. Visit www.rac.co.uk or www.theaa.com for more information.

The bottom line: All businesses need to be prepared for some degree of logistics disruption. This chapter helps you assess how your business may be affected. (If you just want to know about popping over to Europe in the family car, check out the sidebar "Driving the family car in Europe after Brexit.")

Looking at Big-Picture Logistics Issues

In this section, I walk you through some of the wider issues currently impacting the transport and logistics industry in the UK.

Coping with a massive shortage of drivers

Until self-driving trucks become the norm and we all accept the dominance of our machine overlords, the movement of goods around the UK and across Europe still relies on human drivers. Yet, the industry is already experiencing a significant shortage of drivers for heavy goods vehicles (HGVs), also known as large goods vehicles (LGVs).

REMEMBER

In 2018, the shortage of HGV drivers was estimated at more than 50,000, meaning there were more than 50,000 vacancies for HGV drivers in the UK. And it looks like the situation may get worse.

According to the 2018 Moore Stephens/Barclays UK Logistics Confidence Index — which registered a big decline in confidence in the industry in 2018 — one in five UK logistics companies were expecting their driver numbers to drop across the following year, as a result of older drivers retiring and drivers from the EU choosing to work elsewhere (thanks, in part, to the weaker pound).

Data from the Confederation of British Industry (CBI) shows that 14 percent of HGV/LGV drivers in the UK are EU nationals. What's more, 60 percent of drivers in the UK logistics industry are 45 or older.

REMEMBER

Within this landscape of an aging workforce, European drivers being less attracted to working in the UK, and an already large shortage of drivers, it's no wonder that more than half of the companies surveyed for the UK Logistics Confidence Index said a driver shortage was their top business concern. And that's *before* you factor ongoing Brexit uncertainty into the mix.

Maintaining access to workers in the logistics sector

Figures from the Freight Transport Association (FTA) in 2018, show that the UK logistics sector is heavily reliant on access to workers from Europe. The figures are pretty eye-opening:

>> There are 43,000 HGV drivers from Europe working in the UK.

>> There are 113,000 European warehouse workers in the UK.

>> There are 22,000 van drivers from Europe working in the UK.

REMEMBER

In an industry that's already under intense pressure due to a shortage of drivers, there are huge concerns that Brexit will restrict access to non-UK workers. If those fears are realized, it could lead to major disruption to supply chains right across the UK, and an increase in employment costs (essentially, paying more to attract workers). Rising costs will be passed onto customers, which means increased costs for businesses that transport (and store) goods, even if you transport goods only within the UK.

So, when the UK government announced its plans to stop giving EU workers preferential access to the UK jobs market, and prioritize skilled workers from anywhere in the world earning £30,000 a year or more, the logistics industry responded harshly. (See Part 2 for more on UK–EU negotiations and what Brexit means for the free movement of people.)

The FTA's head of skills, Sally Gilson, was quoted as saying that without easy access to non-UK workers, "schools, shops, hospitals and retailers, as well as manufacturers and homeowners, will all find it harder to access the goods they need in order to conduct their daily lives."

Sure, in an ideal world, logistics vacancies in the UK could be easily filled by UK citizens, by attracting school and college leavers, targeting people who want a change of career, or targeting areas of high unemployment.

But in the real world, the physical location of logistics vacancies often doesn't correspond with high-unemployment areas. And the truth is, many British workers are simply attracted to other career paths. That's why, just as in the agriculture sector, the logistics industry has come to rely on non-UK workers, benefiting, in particular, from easy access to EU workers.

REMEMBER

In response to the government's immigration plan, the FTA was quick to point out that many workers coming from Europe fill positions in low-unemployment areas, where competition for workers is already high.

Relying solely on UK employees in these low-unemployment areas could spell disaster for logistics companies — because competing for a smaller pool of UK employees in a low-unemployment area invariably means having to offer higher salaries to fill positions. That's if UK workers can even be tempted to switch careers. . . .

And so we come back to the government's plan to allow unskilled workers from the EU visa-free access to the UK jobs market for a 12-month period. (Circle back to Part 2 for more on the movement of people after Brexit, and see Chapter 7 for guidance on employing EU citizens after Brexit.)

Initially, this low-skilled worker scheme was targeted specifically at agriculture and other related sectors. However, given the outcry from the logistics sector, the government may move to include transport and logistics workers in this scheme (notwithstanding the point that HGV drivers are obviously skilled, qualified workers!). What is clear is that the logistics industry is pushing hard to retain easy access to European workers.

Rising demand for warehousing

In the months leading up to the originally intended date for the UK's departure from the EU (March 29, 2019), warehousing operators reported a surge in Brexit-related demand.

In January 2019, the UK Warehousing Association (UKWA), reported the following:

>> Three-quarters of warehousing operators in the UK were operating at full capacity and unable to take on new business.

>> Eighty-five percent of warehouses had received warehousing enquiries that were related to Brexit concerns.

>> Storage costs had shot up by 25 percent in just three months.

In effect, businesses across the country were seeking additional storage so that they could stockpile goods and spare parts wherever possible, in the event of a no-deal Brexit and delays at British ports. Companies as diverse as Bentley, GlaxoSmithKline and Premier Foods (which includes Mr Kipling's cakes) all confirmed they were planning to stockpile goods in the run-up to Brexit.

This will no doubt come as a relief to generations of Brits who have been raised on Mr Kipling's Battenberg, Cherry Bakewells, and Viennese Whirls. Even if we can't have our figurative Brexit cake and eat it, too, we can at least continue to have our literal cake and eat it!

REMEMBER

This capacity crisis, according to the UKWA, was exacerbated by the fact that few developers were building new warehouse space, as well as a labor shortage in warehousing (again, because of EU workers choosing to return home or work in another EU country). The UKWA chief executive, Peter Ward, described it as "a perfect storm in the warehousing and logistics industry."

Spotting the opportunities for the UK logistics sector

If this all sounds a bit doom and gloom, there are some bright spots emerging from the logistics industry. For example, many transport firms are investing in new technology like big data analytics and artificial intelligence to help them plan more efficient routes, maintain a more efficient fleet of vehicles, and ensure that vehicles are operating at maximum capacity.

The hope is that this approach will help to reduce transportation costs for logistics companies and the businesses they serve. Unfortunately, those companies that are unwilling or unable to invest in new technologies may experience trading difficulties, become uncompetitive, and risk being left behind.

In addition, Brexit may result in reduced competition from EU-based transport and logistics companies, opening up new market opportunities for British firms.

Preparing for More Stringent Border Controls

Now that you have a handle on the big-picture issues facing the logistics sector, this section explains what all this may mean for your business, whether you run a logistics company, you're a florist, you're an online retailer, or something else.

Assessing the timeline for change

If the UK government agrees on a withdrawal deal, which includes a transition period, then it'll be business as usual in terms of the flow of goods for the duration of the transition period, while the longer-term arrangement is negotiated.

However, if no withdrawal deal is agreed upon and the UK crashes out of the EU with no transition period, then — literally overnight — the process for border checks would, in theory, have to change as soon as the UK exits the EU.

Being ready for increased border checks

Even if the UK authorities are able to agree on a withdrawal agreement, and secure a free-trade agreement with their EU counterparts in the long term, it's still likely that border controls may change in one way or another.

For goods entering and exiting the UK, moving to and from Europe, this may mean increased paperwork, potentially new customs duties, and stricter checks on the goods being transported. Circle back to Chapter 5 to read more about the paperwork and customs payments side of things (including the potential impact on value-added tax [VAT]).

REMEMBER

This situation is likely to lead to delays at borders as officials check that goods entering the EU from the UK (and vice versa) have the correct paperwork. The government has pledged that, in the event of a no-deal Brexit, it would minimize customs checks on goods arriving from Europe at the UK border as much as possible. But it has no control over how the EU decides to apply border checks. (See the section "Factoring in potential delays at the border and en route" coming up next.)

On certain cross-channel routes between France, Belgium, and the UK (such as the Eurotunnel route between Folkestone and Calais, and the ferry routes among Dover and Calais and Dunkirk), *juxtaposed border controls* apply. This system allows the participating countries to conduct their border control checks before vehicles board the ferry or train (as opposed to when they disembark on the other side, as in normal border controls). In layman's terms, this means that UK officials are able to conduct border controls in, say, Calais *before* vehicles reach the UK, and French officials can conduct their customs checks in, say, Folkestone, before vehicles arrive in mainland Europe. This system has worked perfectly well, and it ensures a smooth passage of vehicles and minimal delays.

So, will this system continue after Brexit? We don't know, and it potentially depends upon what's agreed on in future trade negotiations (see Chapter 4). However, it's worth noting that the Netherlands is likely to join the juxtaposed control system, to cover direct train journeys between the UK and the Netherlands. In other words, the system looks like it's set to expand, so it makes little sense to scrap it altogether.

Factoring in potential delays at the border and en route

Any introduction of increased checks on paperwork and goods at borders will probably mean delays for goods entering and exiting the UK.

Assessing the impact on UK ports

This will be felt keenly at ports like Dover, which is the UK's biggest port for *roll-on/roll-off ferries* (meaning cargo is driven onto the ship instead of being craned on in shipping containers). On these short crossings, where the volume of traffic is extremely high, even brief delays have the potential to cause chaos.

REMEMBER

In 2018, Dover handled 2.9 million units of roll-on/roll-off freight, with the vast majority of these units being trucks. For goods traveling to and from the EU prior to Brexit, these trucks could simply be driven onto the ferry without having to wait for customs checks. This means 11,000 trucks can pass through the port each day, with each one typically being processed within two minutes.

Start introducing customs checks for these vehicles, and you're looking at potentially huge delays. Checking documents can delay a vehicle by as much as one to three hours, while physically inspecting the goods inside can take even longer. Some estimates have suggested up to eight hours for this process *per vehicle.*

One often-quoted statistic coming from Brexiteers is that customs checks for vehicles arriving into the port of Southampton from outside the EU take only six seconds, so why should we panic about EU goods potentially being subject to the same sort of checks? But, in fact, that statistic is rather misleading. Customs declarations are processed at Southampton within an average of six seconds, but that's not the same as goods being cleared for customs. Typically, it takes a full hour for the goods to go through customs clearance at Southampton — and that's only if all the right paperwork has all been completed in advance.

Add an hour onto the processing time for trucks going in and out of Dover and — because of the frequency of Dover ferry crossings and the sheer volume of trucks passing through the port each day — we could see significant traffic jams choking up the motorways in Kent, and delays on the movement of goods. Even if the UK waves through EU trucks heading into the UK, assuming the EU is conducting its own customs checks on UK vehicles, it'll still mean delays.

Motorists in Kent will bear the brunt of this — the motorways surrounding Dover will become parking lots for waiting trucks. But businesses around the country will also suffer if they have to wait for their goods to arrive, run out of stock, or are late delivering to customers.

REMEMBER

The UK government is also introducing a new Customs Declaration System (CDS) for UK importing and exporting companies, which will replace the long-running Customs Handling of Import and Export Freight (CHIEF) system. Full implementation of CDS was delayed, meaning it may now clash with Britain's exit from the

EU — and if that happens, it may heap further misery on strained ports. Visit www.gov.uk/guidance/how-hmrc-will-introduce-the-customs-declaration-service to stay up to date on the latest CDS developments.

Away from Dover, at other major ports like Southampton, Felixstowe, and London Gateway, 90 percent of goods are either coming from or going to non-EU destinations, so it's hoped the disruption at these locations may be minimal.

TIP

Stay up to date on the latest government advice regarding changes at the UK–EU border. Visit www.gov.uk/government/publications/partnership-pack-preparing-for-a-no-deal-eu-exit to read more.

Will there be further delays when trucks get through customs?

After trucks have actually made it through ports and are on their way to their final destination, they may still experience delays traveling through Europe.

REMEMBER

Haulage companies have already been reporting increased spot checks on British vehicles driving in the EU, checking vehicle registration documents, and so on. After the UK has left the EU, it's fair to expect these sorts of spot checks to continue or increase, particularly if the UK and EU diverge on rules like maximum working hours.

Considering the impact on European businesses

In addition to all the disruption this could bring to the UK supply chain, it's worth noting that many European companies rely on the UK for major parts of their supply chain.

There's also the fact that food exported to the UK by EU counterparts would literally rot during transport in the event of significant delays. We're talking about millions and millions of pounds of perishable goods, so either way the UK and the EU will need to find a suitable answer.

What about goods crossing the land border between Northern Ireland and the Republic of Ireland?

We know that the Northern Ireland "backstop" — and in general the need to avoid a hard border between Northern Ireland and the Republic of Ireland — was a huge bone of contention during the UK–EU withdrawal negotiations (see Part 2).

The effect of Brexit on the peace process across Northern Ireland and the Republic of Ireland is beyond the scope of this chapter, although it's obviously a major concern for all parties — Northern Ireland, the rest of the UK, the Republic of Ireland, and the EU. Let's look instead at what may change for goods crossing the border between the two countries.

If a withdrawal agreement, including a transition period, is agreed, then in the short term nothing will change. Goods and people will still be able to move freely across the border without any kind of checks. Any longer-term arrangement will have to be agreed upon by both parties as part of ongoing trade negotiations. (See Chapter 3 for more on the "backstop" and the Northern Ireland border.)

REMEMBER

In the less likely event of a no-deal Brexit, things get much stickier. After the withdrawal agreement was rejected by Parliament for a second time in March 2019 (see Chapter 3), the UK government released a plan to manage the border in the event of a no-deal Brexit. According to this plan, for a temporary period, there would be no new checks or controls at the border, and goods arriving into Northern Ireland from Ireland wouldn't be subject to new tariffs. But this is only temporary, and a permanent solution would still need to be negotiated with the EU.

The government has also proposed that a technologically advanced, nonphysical border could be implemented to track the flow of goods — which, theoretically could involve using satellites to monitor border crossings and a computer system to allow goods to be declared before they leave warehouses. Unfortunately, at the moment, the technology doesn't really exist to do this, meaning it could only ever be considered as a very long-term, highly theoretical solution.

And let's remember that the UK government's plan is only half the story; EU rules would obviously apply for goods flowing in the reverse direction, from Northern Ireland (part of the UK) into Ireland (part of the EU). One big concern is that, without border checks, goods could illegally enter the EU via Northern Ireland. So, in theory, Ireland would need to check goods arriving from the UK, which would involve some form of border presence. At the time of writing, it's unclear how this will play out in practice.

What Happens When Your Delivery Vehicles Travel in Europe?

According to government advice published in March 2019, once the UK leaves the EU (regardless of whether we exit with a deal or no deal):

>> Commercial trailers weighing over 750 kilograms (1,653 pounds) and noncommercial trailers weighing over 3,500 kilograms (7,716 pounds) will need to be registered with the Driver and Vehicle Licensing Agency (DVLA) before traveling abroad.

>> Drivers towing these trailers will need to carry the trailer registration certificate and trailer registration plates.

In the event of a no-deal Brexit:

>> UK haulage drivers will need to carry International Driving Permits (IDPs) and motor insurance Green Cards, and display a GB sticker on the backs of their vehicles.

>> UK haulage drivers can continue to use their EU Community Licenses until December 31, 2019 (this date may be subject to change).

>> It's not yet clear whether UK haulage drivers may need to exchange their UK Driver Certificates of Professional Competence (CPCs) for an EU CPC if they drive in Europe.

All the above is in addition to any extra customs paperwork that may be required for the goods being transported (see Chapter 5). And haulage drivers will continue to need to carry their vehicle registration documents and passports as before.

WARNING

Haulage companies must be aware of the paperwork required for their vehicles traveling in Europe. Confusion regarding the exact information needed to travel across Europe could lead to significant penalties and maybe even the removal of vehicles from the road.

TIP

These lists are up to date at the time of writing but, like lots of things to do with Brexit, are subject to change. The following sites will help you stay up to date on the latest documentation required for HGV drivers driving in Europe:

>> **Prepare to drive in the EU after Brexit:** www.gov.uk/guidance/prepare-to-drive-in-the-eu-after-brexit-lorry-and-goods-vehicle-drivers

>> **Transport goods out of the UK by road if the UK leaves the EU without a deal:** www.gov.uk/guidance/transport-goods-out-of-the-uk-by-road-if-the-uk-leaves-the-eu-without-a-deal-checklist-for-hauliers

It's also a good idea to sign up for DVLA email alerts at https://public.govdelivery.com/accounts/UKDVLA/subscriber/new.

Planning for Potential Supply Chain Disruption

To summarize the potential disruption UK businesses may face:

>> Goods may be subject to increased customs checks as they cross a UK–EU border.

>> Haulage drivers and vehicles may be subject to stricter documentation checks, both at the border and while driving through Europe.

>> We may see delays at UK ports like Dover, meaning it may take longer to transport goods in and out of the UK. And this may impact goods being transported within the UK if vehicles and drivers are held up elsewhere.

>> Warehousing is already in higher demand as businesses have been looking to stockpile goods in preparation for disruption.

>> All this comes amidst a shortage of qualified HGV drivers in the EU and potentially limited access to logistics workers from the EU.

REMEMBER

However Brexit pans out — whether there are major traffic jams at ports, ferries being canceled, or minimal disruption — there are still likely to be some teething problems as the UK and EU adjust to their new relationship. Therefore, whether you own or work for a logistics company or a nonlogistics company, it's wise to prepare for potential supply chain disruption.

TIP

In Chapter 9, I provide checklists to help you conduct a Brexit impact assessment for your business.

Coping with higher transport and storage costs

Given all that I outline in this chapter, it's likely that the costs associated with transporting and storing goods will increase due to factors such as the following:

>> The existing shortage of haulage drivers is already putting a strain on transportation companies, forcing many to increase prices.

>> Difficulties in recruiting labor going forward may mean logistics companies have to pay more to attract staff — a cost that'll be passed on to customers.

>> Fuel expenses and journey times will increase for transportation companies if their vehicles sit idle in traffic lines at ports.

>> Additional customs paperwork (see Chapter 5) will create an extra administrative burden for logistics companies and their clients, which will invariably mean higher costs.

Any increase in costs will impact a business's bottom line, so it's important that companies manage their costs carefully (which may mean looking for new suppliers), maximize cash flow wherever possible, and plan for future increases in costs as early as possible.

Being ready for potential delays

Be sure to update your website, terms and conditions, and service contracts in line with changes in anticipated delivery times. If you know it's going to take longer to deliver items to your end customers, you must communicate that clearly.

And if unexpected, one-off delays arise on a particular delivery, be sure to communicate openly and clearly with your customers on what's happening, what you're doing to resolve the situation, and when you expect it to be resolved.

TIP

If you bring stock in from the EU, be prepared to work to longer lead times than you may be used to. Wherever possible, you may choose to stockpile items to help counter supply chain delays.

Communicating with your logistics suppliers

In the run-up to and aftermath of Brexit, companies must keep an open line of communication with their logistics suppliers (and vice versa — logistics companies need to keep their clients up to date on the latest events and what it means for their services).

TIP

Turn to Chapter 10 for helpful ideas on how to protect your business against Brexit uncertainty, including communicating with your suppliers and customers.

Transporting Goods to and from Non-EU Countries

If you transport goods to and from non-EU countries, it'll be business as usual for your logistics — at least in terms of customs procedures.

WARNING

However, you may be affected by delays at UK ports. Therefore, even if you don't transport goods to and from the EU, even if you only deal with non-EU destinations, be prepared for potential delays and rising costs.

IN THIS CHAPTER

» Looking at the wider implications of Brexit for UK employment law

» Understanding how Brexit affects your existing European employees

» Providing support for employees (European and otherwise) through uncertain times

» Ensuring continued access to the labor you need after Brexit

» Sizing up changes for British citizens working in Europe

» Tackling short-term business trips to Europe

Chapter 7

Employing EU Citizens in the UK (And Vice Versa)

Ask a group of business leaders to list their company's core assets and you may get some very different answers. Some may focus on tangible business assets, such as buildings, land, cash in the bank, equipment, stock inventory, and so on. Others may prioritize less tangible assets, like patents, customer data, brand recognition, and so on. What one business considers valuable may be less vital to another business.

But there's one asset that pretty much all business leaders agree on — one asset that's extremely critical to the value of any business, regardless of its size or industry. That asset is *people*. From frontline employees to the leadership team, people are what makes a business work, grow, and succeed.

That's why Brexit has many business leaders concerned. Some may be worried about the potential loss of individual European employees and the valuable skills they bring to the company; others who are absolutely reliant on workers from abroad face potentially huge staffing headaches as the free movement of people between the UK and Europe comes to an end.

In this chapter, I look at the impact of Brexit on employees, access to labor, and bigger-picture employment issues in the UK.

Looking at the Big Picture: How Will Brexit Affect Employment Law?

Much of the UK's existing employment law is borne out of EU regulations. Some Brexiteers suggested that Brexit would trigger a "bonfire" of regulation, with pesky EU rules and red tape being ripped up left, right, and center, but it's highly unlikely that'll play out in real life.

REMEMBER

Although Prime Minister Theresa May promised Parliament a say on which EU employment rules to keep in the UK, in reality, UK employment law will most likely stay broadly the same, at least in the short and medium term. For one thing, UK employment law is enshrined in UK regulations or Acts of Parliament, and immediately undoing all that would be a bureaucratic nightmare.

Sticking with the EU on most areas

Even in the longer term, most areas of UK employment law that abide by EU rules are unlikely to change drastically, and the UK will probably end up largely complying with EU employment law.

REMEMBER

That's because any trade deal that's agreed between the UK and EU as part of our "future relations" negotiations (see Chapter 4) may contain stipulations that the UK will abide by certain EU employment law.

It's also worth remembering that there are some areas of UK employment law that go above and beyond the EU's position — maternity leave and annual leave being two prime examples.

Where might the UK disagree with EU law?

After Brexit, it'll be up to Parliament to decide whether certain aspects of employment law and employment rights will change. This has some people concerned that the UK government may move to restrict certain workers' rights.

One area that may be a real bone of contention is the 48-hour week. Under EU law, workers can't work more than 48 hours a week on average, which includes overtime.

This is one area where the UK chose to depart from EU rules, even before the Brexit vote. Under UK employment law, people can choose to opt out of this 48-hour limit, meaning someone who wants to put in more hours can do so legally. (Many would question whether it's really the employee's "choice" to opt out if he's under pressure from his employer and worried about losing his job, but that's another story.)

REMEMBER

Some sources predict that the UK government may look to abolish the 48-hour maximum workweek altogether after Brexit. This would mean that there would be no upper limit on working hours, and an employer could force employees to work, say, 50-hour weeks, whether those employees wanted to or not.

This would prompt a fierce battle with unions in the UK, so there's no saying the move would definitely go ahead. However, it shows that the UK may look to distance itself from EU employment law in some areas. And if the UK did go ahead with such a move, it could become a sticking point in future negotiations between the UK and the EU.

There have also been suggestions that the UK government might look to change the rules on collective redundancies. At the time of writing, current UK employment law states that if a company wants to make 20 or more employees redundant, "collective redundancy" obligations are triggered, which means the employer has to go through a formal period of consultation with staff representatives. The government may look to increase this 20-employee threshold, making it easier for employers to make large numbers of people redundant without triggering consultations.

So British workers might end up with fewer protections?

In theory, yes. Although, the specifics will be dictated by the in-depth UK–EU negotiations that begin after Brexit. (Remember that Theresa May's withdrawal agreement only covers the UK's exit from the EU — almost every aspect of the

UK's ongoing relationship with the EU has yet to be decided. See Chapters 3 and 4 for more about this.)

Former Brexit Secretary David Davis made an interesting point about workers' rights in 2016. Writing for the Conservative Home website, he said:

> Empirical studies show that it is not employment regulation that stultifies economic growth. . . . Britain has a relatively flexible workforce, and so long as the employment law environment stays reasonably stable, it should not be a problem for business. . . . There is also a political or perhaps sentimental point. The great British industrial working classes voted overwhelmingly for Brexit. I am not at all attracted by the idea of rewarding them by cutting their rights.

Basically, Davis was acknowledging that many of the UK working class voted in favor of Brexit, so it makes no sense to deprive them of precious employment law protections. Many people voted for Brexit because they believed it would help Britons lead more prosperous lives. Taking away employment protections would hardly deliver that.

Managing the Impact on Your Existing European Employees

As of this writing, it looks very likely that Brexit will prompt a change in UK immigration rules, as, under the terms of Theresa May's withdrawal agreement (Chapter 3) and political declaration on future UK–EU relations (Chapter 4) free movement of people between the EU and the UK will end. So, what does this mean for your employees who hail from Europe? Read on to find out.

Recognizing the contribution of EU citizens to the UK economy

As of 2017, there were 3.8 million people living in the UK who were born in *EU27 countries* (the 27 remaining members of the EU after Brexit). Many of them are gainfully employed and contributing to the success of UK businesses. (Many are self-employed, too.) In fact, EU citizens living in the UK are *net contributors* to UK public finances (see Chapter 2), meaning they pay more into the UK system through taxes than they take out in benefits, healthcare, and so on. And let's not forget that certain industries in the UK are absolutely reliant on workers coming from overseas, especially from Europe.

REMEMBER

Given all this, it was always highly unlikely that the UK was going to "kick out" the millions of Europeans who have settled and built lives for themselves in the UK. The rights of EU citizens in the UK (and vice versa) was, therefore, one of the earliest things agreed in the withdrawal negotiations.

Making sure employees secure "settled status" in the UK

Under the terms of Theresa May's withdrawal agreement, EU citizens already living in the UK prior to Brexit (and any who move during the transition period) will retain the right to stay on in the UK and have their existing rights and entitlements protected until the end of the transition period (currently set to end on December 31, 2020, but this may change as the Brexit date keeps being pushed back).

REMEMBER

However, EU citizens living in the UK will have to apply for settled status if they want to continue living and working in the UK after the transition period ends. *Settled status* is the name given to the government scheme that provides security for EU nationals living in the UK, allowing them to stay on indefinitely.

Therefore, your EU national employees will need to obtain settled status if they want to remain in the UK indefinitely. Here are the key points to note on obtaining settled status:

>> Eligibility for settled status applies to EU nationals who have been resident in the UK for five years.

>> Those who have lived here for less than five years needn't worry. They apply for *pre-settled status,* which gives them the right to stay in the UK until they reach their five years' residency. At which point, they'll be eligible to apply for settled status.

>> As of this writing, the cutoff point to apply for the settlement scheme is June 30, 2021.

>> The scheme applies to EU workers and their families.

>> Those who already have a permanent residence document will still need to apply for settled status or pre-settled status.

>> Those who have indefinite leave to enter or indefinite leave to remain, or British or Irish citizenship (including dual citizenship), do *not* have to apply for settled status. They'll be covered by their existing status.

You or your employees can find out more about the settlement scheme and apply for settled or pre-settled status at www.gov.uk/settled-status-eu-citizens-families. There's also a helpful employer toolkit for the settlement scheme, available at www.gov.uk/government/publications/eu-settlement-scheme-employer-toolkit.

In the unlikely event that the UK leaves the EU without agreeing to a withdrawal deal ("no-deal Brexit"), then the transition period will no longer apply, and only those EU nationals already living in the UK prior to the exit date will be able to apply for settled and pre-settled status. At the time of writing, the deadline for applying is set as December 31, 2020.

Obviously, this may be a confusing and anxious time for employees who hail from Europe. It's, therefore, vital that employers support their employees (European and otherwise) through Brexit uncertainty.

Supporting All Your Employees through Uncertain Times

Whether your company employs lots of EU citizens or none at all, Brexit disruption and uncertainty may have an indirect effect on employee engagement and performance.

Regardless of where they were born, your employees may be worried about their jobs, be concerned how processes and roles may change, or simply be unclear how the business as a whole may be affected by Brexit. This uncertainty can breed significant problems from a people-management perspective.

Considering the effect of disruption on the workforce

Writing for *Personnel Today* in March 2019, Brian Kropp, Group Vice President of Research and Consultancy firm Gartner, noted that two negative trends tend to occur during times of business disruption:

>> Employee engagement dips, and high-potential employees are more likely to quit.

>> Employees are more likely to demonstrate problematic behaviors, including lying, stealing, and cheating. In fact, "bad behavior" increases up to 33 percent during times of major disruption.

REMEMBER

That last point may surprise you. Many business leaders tend to assume that in times of disruption or uncertainty, employees will dig deep and "knuckle down" — that they'll engage more deeply with the business and raise their performance levels in order to keep the business functioning and secure their own jobs. But Gartner's historical analysis shows that the opposite is true.

Common sense says we should want to hang onto our jobs when times get tough, right? In theory, that makes sense. But humans are, well, human. We don't always behave the way we should. (If we did, there'd be no crime, war, poverty, or *X Factor*.)

WARNING

Gartner's historical data shows how assumptions of employee loyalty during difficult times are totally misplaced. If we look back to the financial crisis of 2008, observed cases of employee misconduct shot up by one-third between the first and third quarters of 2008. Theft, fraud, bogus injury claims, and generally unethical behavior can all spike when uncertainty strikes.

Problematic behavior in the workplace and reduced employee engagement have a drastic impact on productivity and performance:

>> In times of disruption and uncertainty, an "information vacuum" often develops, meaning employers reduce or close off the lines of communication between the company and its employees (often because the company feels unable to give definitive answers or reassurance). This is extremely dangerous. When you leave an information vacuum like this, people tend to fill in the blanks with their own assumptions and predictions.

>> If employees are unsure about the company's future, they're more likely to seek "secure" employment elsewhere. For employees from the EU, this may mean returning home. But even for those employees who are British born and bred, the temptation can be very strong to look for employment in a company that's (seemingly) less affected by disruption.

>> In the wake of the 2008 financial crisis, employees' need for recognition (be it through compensation, praise, or other means of recognition) rose significantly. In other words, when times get tough, employees want to know that their employer values them. If their employer doesn't deliver that increased recognition, they can disengage, look for employment elsewhere, or demonstrate problematic behavior.

>> In addition to these reasons, Brexit brings an added layer of complexity, particularly for any employees from the EU. They may have huge concerns about their future in the UK, or they may feel like they're no longer welcome in a country that voted to end free movement from Europe. Remember that the referendum was extremely divisive (see Chapter 2 for a recap of the key issues in the referendum) — instead of putting the issue of Europe "to bed," it ended up igniting fierce division in society.

Taking practical steps to engage and retain your employees

If you want to avoid losing high-potential employees, maintain levels of engagement and performance, and nip the chance of problematic behavior in the bud, what should you do?

TIP

The following strategies will help you support your employees through difficult times. They can be applied to pretty much any period of business disruption, beyond Brexit.

>> **First thing's first, you must monitor employee engagement closely.** You can't manage what you don't measure! Regularly take the temperature of your staff so that you can spot any shifts in engagement levels and take swift action.

>> **If you haven't already implemented regular updates about the impact of Brexit on the business, now is the time to start.** These updates could be in the form of a regular email, guidance document, or face-to-face briefing sessions. Even if there's nothing much to say, or even if you don't have all the answers at this stage, you must keep the lines of communication open. Be upfront about any uncertainties and gray areas, and reassure employees that you're on top of the situation.

>> **Communicate clearly with EU citizen employees regarding their rights and entitlements to remain in the UK.** Reassure them that they're welcome and valued. And if you have the means, offer them access to legal advice and/ or support with completing the necessary paperwork.

>> **Give employees a forum to ask their Brexit-related questions.** Encourage them to talk to their line manager about their concerns. Have an anonymous question box or page on the company intranet where staff can pose questions and get answers. Or why not hold a regular company-wide Q&A session?

>> **Be wary of leaning too heavily on key staff, letting star performers bear the brunt of disruption or business change.** Expecting reliable, valuable employees to take on increased workloads, particularly if that's not reflected in their paycheck, can spread discontent in the workplace.

>> **Be on the lookout for signs of prejudice, discrimination, or friction between British and European employees.** Get immediate advice from your HR team or adviser if you have any concerns about discrimination.

>> **Reward your people for a job well done, especially if their job has become harder or their workload has increased as a result of Brexit.** If financial rewards are out of the question, remember that simple praise and recognition go a long way.

>> **Constantly reinforce the company's values and the standards of behavior expected by everyone in the business.** And remember that these values, best practices, ethical behavior, and so on must be modeled from the top down. In other words, "Do as I say" won't cut the mustard; it's a case of "Do as I do."

ADVICE FOR EUROPEAN CITIZENS ALREADY LIVING AND WORKING IN THE UK

If you're an EU national already living in the UK prior to the UK's exit from the EU, you'll be able to stay on indefinitely providing you apply for settled or pre-settled status. (See the section "Making sure employees secure settled status in the UK," earlier in the chapter.) In most cases, you'll also be able to apply for British citizenship 12 months after obtaining settled status, if that's something that appeals to you.

The same settlement scheme applies to EU citizens who move to the UK before the Brexit date or before the end of any transition period (currently set to end on December 31, 2020, but this date may change).

Read more about the UK government's settlement scheme and apply for settled or pre-settled status at www.gov.uk/settled-status-eu-citizens-families.

Don't be afraid to ask your employer for the support you need during this process. The internal HR team may be able to provide guidance, or put you in touch with appropriate external organizations that offer independent advice.

Making Sure You Have Ongoing Access to the Labor You Need

So far in this chapter, we've looked at the impact on existing employees and those European citizens already living in the UK. But what happens if you want to take on new employees from the EU after Brexit? What happens, for example, if your business relies on seasonal workers coming from the EU for a few months at a time.

Understanding immigration changes after Brexit

Under the terms of Theresa May's withdrawal agreement, freedom of movement will remain in place for the duration of the transition period. So, if that agreement is approved by the UK Parliament, then, in the very short term, the ability of UK businesses to recruit from the EU won't change.

REMEMBER

However, after the transition period ends, according to the Conservative government's plans, the process for EU citizens coming to work in the UK (and vice versa), will fall under new, more complicated immigration rules. (In the event of a no-deal Brexit, there'd be no transitional period at all, and EU citizens would be subject to new immigration rules right away.) Effectively, the UK's new immigration approach means that skilled EU workers will be subject to the same immigration policy and rules as workers coming from the rest of the world. There'll be no preferential treatment for those coming from the EU.

The UK government is currently talking about a skilled employment threshold of £30,000, meaning those coming to work in the UK, whether they're from Europe or anywhere else in the world, must secure a wage of £30,000 or above to gain entry.

There has been a lot of backlash against this proposal, and it's not yet clear whether the plans will go ahead. (If they do go ahead, the threshold could be adjusted depending on the specific skill sets required at the time.) One of the main objections is that certain sectors in the UK, including the National Health Service (NHS) and agriculture, rely on easy access to workers from the EU who don't earn anywhere near £30,000 a year.

REMEMBER

That's why the government has unveiled plans for unskilled workers from "low-risk countries" (likely to include all of the EU) to be allowed to come and work in the UK for up to 12 months without needing a visa. In theory, this means that care homes, hospitals, farms, and other employers who rely on easy access to

European workers will still have access to the labor they need to survive. The idea is to avoid employee shortages wherever possible.

Workers coming to the UK on this 12-month, visa-free scheme will not be able to bring their families to live with them or access public funds (such as benefits) for the duration of their stay. The scheme will apply even if there's a no-deal Brexit, and it's scheduled to last until 2025 (after which point, it'll probably be extended or replaced with something very similar).

Looking at wider trends in access to labor

Initial indications suggest that the proposed unskilled worker system would attract a similar number of EU workers as seen in the UK today. So, in theory, businesses won't suffer negative consequences when it comes to attracting workers from the EU.

REMEMBER

However, in practice, it may not be that simple. Figures released by the Office for National Statistics in November 2018 showed that the number of EU nationals working in the UK had dropped at the fastest rate since records began (in 1997). There were 132,000 fewer EU nationals working in the UK compared to the same period one year earlier. In particular, there had been a massive decline in workers coming from eastern and central European countries, including Bulgaria, Romania, and Poland.

What's more, sectors such as hospitality, healthcare, construction, and agriculture were reporting shortages in workers in 2018.

A number of factors contributed to this decline in EU workers coming to the UK:

>> Socially, the UK is seen by some as a less attractive destination, where EU workers are less "welcome."

>> The weaker pound means workers sending money back to Europe will be worse off. As a result, many prefer to earn their money in other European countries, especially considering the lower cost of living in many European countries.

>> Ongoing political and economic uncertainty makes the UK a less attractive option compared to the remaining EU27 countries.

Therefore, if you're recruiting regularly from the EU, you may need to work harder to attract EU nationals in the future. For many businesses, unfortunately, this means offering higher wages.

Employing UK Citizens in Europe

Although most of this chapter is focused on the impact of Brexit on employees in the UK, it's worth taking a quick timeout to consider the potential impact on British citizens who are employed (or hoping to be employed) in Europe.

REMEMBER

At the time of writing, the intention of the UK government is that free movement between Europe and the UK will end after any transition period (see Chapter 3), but the flip side of this is that people from the UK will no longer have free, unrestricted access to the European labor market. Let's unpack what this may mean for British workers.

What happens to Brits already living and working abroad?

Under the terms of Theresa May's withdrawal agreement (see Chapter 3), UK citizens who are already settled in an EU member state before the end of the transition period will retain their residency rights in the country in which they're settled. Depending on the country, they may have to reapply for their residency (just as most EU nationals living in the UK have to apply for settled status), but the chances of thousands of Brits being unilaterally kicked out of, say, Germany are extremely slim.

In the event of a no-deal Brexit, the picture is less clear, but many EU countries will simply create reciprocal arrangements with the UK, essentially meaning they'll match whatever the UK does for European citizens. However, the arrangements will vary from country to country.

For example, in the event of a no-deal Brexit, UK citizens living in Germany will have three months to register for a new temporary residency permit. This may affect many Brits, as figures suggest there has been a significant increase in the number of British workers moving to Germany since the 2016 Brexit vote. (This phenomenon may be partly connected to the UK's dependence on the German automotive manufacturing industry, or Germany's strong financial sector.)

France, meanwhile, has no plans to impose a visa on British workers, and those already living in France will not need to acquire formal residency. However, this could change and is reliant on the UK government adopting a similar stance with French citizens in the UK.

When it comes to the Republic of Ireland, the "common travel area," which ensures free movement of people between the UK and Ireland, will continue to apply after Brexit.

What happens to Brits who want to move to Europe in the future?

REMEMBER

Assuming the UK exits under the terms of a withdrawal agreement, then after the transition period has ended, any new arrangements (which have yet to be formally agreed upon) would come into play for Brits seeking work in Europe. We don't yet know what these arrangements will look like, but, just as for EU workers coming to work in the UK, it'll likely involve UK citizens having to apply for working visas before they can live and work in the EU.

Despite the fact that the EU is negotiating for all member states, we're likely to see an array of separate arrangements between the UK and individual European countries. These agreements will also be reciprocal — or, to put it another way, EU countries may go easy on UK workers applying to live and work in their country if the UK goes easy on their citizens applying for employment in the UK. You scratch our backs, we'll scratch yours. . . .

Understanding the broader disadvantage for British workers

Ultimately, UK citizens wanting to work in an EU country will have to apply for the right to do so. Assuming they're granted the right to live and work in that European country, the terms of their residency will apply only to that one country. This means they won't be automatically able to work in other European countries; they'd have to apply separately for the right to live and work elsewhere in the EU.

One potential consequence of this is that British candidates may find themselves at a disadvantage compared to European candidates, who are freely able to work right across Europe.

REMEMBER

In theory, candidates from the EU will be more valuable to certain employers because those European workers would have access to the whole EU market — as well as the UK market, if they apply for eligibility. So, a German with the right to work in the UK, has unrestricted access to 28 labor markets (the EU27, plus the UK), while a Briton working in Germany has unrestricted access to just two labor markets (Germany and the UK).

For some sectors, particularly technology and finance, the ability to move freely across the EU (and the UK, if granted permission) could make European candidates a much more attractive prospect than British candidates. The same goes for any multinational company with offices across Europe — the ability to live and work in any EU country may entice them to favor applicants from within the EU over an otherwise qualified British candidate.

Of course, the end of free movement is what many people voted for. Yet, the big-picture downsides for British workers received little attention during the referendum campaign.

What if Your (UK Citizen) Employees Need to Visit Europe on a Business Trip?

The UK and the EU hope to secure a close trading relationship for the future, one that ensures that trade is as hassle-free as possible.

The same is true for travel arrangements. Under the terms of the political declaration on the UK's future relationship with the EU (see Chapter 4), the UK government and its counterparts in the EU are determined to introduce reciprocal short-term travel arrangements that are as smooth and easy as possible.

Ultimately, both parties want to avoid unnecessary bureaucracy for short-term stays. After all, they'll have their hands full negotiating a trade deal and every other aspect of the UK's ongoing relationship with the EU — the thought of introducing visas for business trips and vacations is a bureaucratic nightmare both sides can do without.

REMEMBER

Therefore, the plan is to allow visa-free travel between the UK and the EU (and vice versa) for up to 90 days at a time, totaling no more than 180 days in a year. That means any of your UK citizen employees visiting Europe on short-term business trips should be able to travel under this arrangement without needing to apply for a visa.

In other words, next year's sales conference in Malta or Marbella or whatever sunny European destination you've chosen, can go ahead without added travel headaches. (Sadly there's no such easy fix for the annual alcohol- and heatstroke-induced headaches, though.)

The same is true for European companies sending European citizen employees to the UK on short-term business trips — there's no need for a visa under the current plans.

WARNING

Make sure your employees are covered by comprehensive travel and health insurance when they travel abroad. Relying on the *European Health Insurance Card* (that little blue card that entitles Brits to state-provided medical treatment in European countries) is no longer an option after Brexit.

IN THIS CHAPTER

» **Looking at the implications for subsidiary businesses and branches based in the EU**

» **Ensuring that your intellectual property is protected after Brexit**

» **Scoping out potential changes in environmental standards**

» **Keeping up to date on product safety standards**

» **Being aware of other legal and regulatory changes that may affect your business**

» **Knowing what happens to your** .eu **domain names**

» **Handling the personal data of your customers in a GDPR-friendly way**

» **Reviewing and updating your business contracts where necessary**

Chapter **8**

Eyeing Other Key Business Considerations

I f you've read any of the other chapters in this part, it'll be clear that Brexit could impact businesses in lots of ways — some small, some large. This chapter outlines other miscellaneous considerations for businesses — covering those issues that don't necessarily fall under the bigger topics already discussed, but nonetheless shouldn't be overlooked.

Some of the topics covered in this chapter (trademarks, for instance) may not be relevant to your business, so feel free to dip into the sections that apply and skip over the bits that don't. In a way, this chapter is like a tin of Quality Street (other assorted boxes of chocolates are available!) — go ahead and pick out your favorite chocolates and leave the unwanted coffee cremes at the bottom. We all do it. . . .

TIP

Turn to Chapter 9 for help with conducting a Brexit impact assessment. There, you can find handy checklists to help you assess the different areas of your business and prepare for any potential effects that Brexit may have on your company.

Preparing for Changes for European Branches and Subsidiaries

At the time of writing, it's difficult to say with any certainty how Brexit will impact British companies with European offices and subsidiaries (and European Union [EU] companies with offices and subsidiaries in the United Kingdom [UK], of course). There are a number of issues that your business may need to take into account.

To be clear on the difference between an overseas branch and an overseas subsidiary, in this instance:

>> A *branch* is a local office of a nonresident company. For example, a UK company may have an office in Germany, but the company itself is registered in the UK. The branch is merely an extension of the UK company, not a separate legal entity.

>> A *subsidiary* is a locally registered, independent legal entity that is owned by another company. For example, a German subsidiary company may be owned by a UK company.

Generally speaking, it's easier to conduct business overseas through a subsidiary, because it's an independent legal entity in that country and, therefore, arguably carries more weight with other service providers, registration bodies, investors, and so on that are also based in that country. But there are various tax and legal implications to both approaches.

WARNING

Always seek specific legal and tax advice on how Brexit may impact your company structure and tax position. Given the level of uncertainty around Brexit, the considerations outlined in the rest of this section are of a high-level nature only.

Looking at big-picture risk factors for companies with overseas branches and subsidiaries

If your company maintains a physical presence in an EU country, whether it's a branch or a subsidiary, you'll need to consider some big-picture risk factors, such as the following:

>> Fluctuations in exchange rates between the pound and the euro (something that you'll already be used to prior to Brexit, but that may be compounded by Brexit)

>> Potential tariffs on goods moving between the UK and the EU (see Chapter 5 for more about tariffs and trade)

>> Increasing bureaucracy associated with doing business in another country, inevitably resulting in higher administrative costs

>> Potential supply chain disruptions and higher costs if you're physically moving goods between one country and another (see Chapter 6 for more on this)

Assessing the impact on EU businesses owned by UK companies/citizens (and vice versa)

When the UK is no longer an EU member state, there will inevitably be some changes in how companies are registered, as well as implications for accounting, tax, and auditing.

REMEMBER

Although no one can say with any certainty how things will pan out, here are some general considerations to keep in mind:

>> UK companies may need to apply on a state-by-state basis to do business in different member states.

>> There may be difficulties in transferring funds between EU and non-EU companies. This flow of funds is extremely simple across EU member states, but after the UK is no longer a member, the flow of funds may be subject to various withholding tax arrangements. Going forward, the UK and the EU may look to agree on reciprocal arrangements to avoid double taxation, but this is an area of significant uncertainty.

>> Some member states may have slightly different rules and regulations for foreign-owned companies, leading to additional testing and certification of products or services.

>> Potential changes in consumer patterns in light of Brexit may mean that some companies see fewer benefits from having European branches or subsidiaries (for example, if UK consumers choose to focus more on home-grown products and services).

>> No more free movement between the UK and the EU could impact the efficient movement of employees across different subsidiaries. This could lead to duplicated jobs in different locations and increased costs.

The changes may be more pronounced and sudden in the (increasingly unlikely) event of a no-deal Brexit. If a no-deal Brexit occurs, the UK government has said the following:

>> UK citizens may face restrictions in their ability to own, manage, or direct companies registered in the EU, depending on the sector and country.

>> UK businesses that own or run business operations in an EU country are likely to face changes to the law under which they operate (again, depending on the sector and the country).

>> UK companies and limited liability partnerships that have their principal place of business or central administration in certain EU member states may no longer have their limited liability recognized.

>> Certain companies may need to change their UK company registrations at Companies House. This applies to European entities formed under EU law (such as Societas Europaea [SE] companies), UK companies with an European Economic Area (EEA; see Chapter 1 for key EU and Brexit definitions) corporate officer, UK companies involved in a cross-border merger, and EEA companies.

>> UK investors may also face restrictions on the amount of equity that they can hold in an EU business, depending on the sector and the country.

WARNING

If your business owns an EU-based subsidiary company, or has a branch based in the EU, take legal advice on what restrictions may apply.

TIP

Stay up to date on the latest government advice for businesses by visiting the following websites:

>> **Structuring your business if there's no Brexit deal:** www.gov.uk/government/publications/structuring-your-business-if-theres-no-brexit-deal--2/structuring-your-business-if-theres-no-brexit-deal

>> **Accounting and audit if there's no Brexit deal:** www.gov.uk/government/publications/accounting-and-audit-if-theres-no-brexit-deal/accounting-and-audit-if-theres-no-brexit-deal

>> **Changing your company registration if the UK leaves the EU without a deal:** www.gov.uk/guidance/changing-your-company-registration-if-the-uk-leaves-the-eu-without-a-deal

>> **Changes to Companies House forms in the event of a no-deal Brexit:** www.gov.uk/guidance/changes-to-companies-house-forms-in-the-event-of-a-no-deal-brexit

Deciding whether to set up an EU subsidiary

Like many businesses, you may be considering whether it's a smart move to set up a European subsidiary company to make trading in Europe easier in the future.

REMEMBER

Ultimately, whether this is the right move for you will depend on what sector you operate in, whether your company is big enough, whether it's commercially viable (that is, whether you do enough business in Europe to warrant it), and whether operating overseas is tax efficient for your business. Because there's so much uncertainty around Brexit, it may be wise to let the dust settle a little, after the UK has left the EU, and then assess the best options for your business.

Of course, this question doesn't only apply to UK companies. If you own a business in the United States, for example, and you have a subsidiary company in the UK, you may need to consider setting up an EU-based subsidiary if you do a lot of business within the EU.

Safeguarding Your Intellectual Property: Copyright, Trademarks, Designs, and Patents

If your business owns intellectual property (IP) — specifically copyright, trademarks, designs, and patents — that IP may be affected by Brexit.

WARNING

The information in this section is intended as a general guide to the various IP considerations. Seek legal advice on how best to protect your IP in the UK and EU, and always stay up to date on the latest government advice by visiting the following websites:

>> **Intellectual Property Office:** www.gov.uk/government/organisations/intellectual-property-office

>> **Intellectual property after Brexit**: www.gov.uk/guidance/intellectual-property-after-brexit

>> **IP and Brexit:** www.gov.uk/government/publications/ip-and-brexit-the-facts

In addition, the following government guidance covers IP in a no-deal scenario:

>> **Copyright if there's no Brexit deal:** www.gov.uk/government/publications/copyright-if-theres-no-brexit-deal/copyright-if-theres-no-brexit-deal

>> **Trademarks and designs if there's no Brexit deal:** www.gov.uk/government/publications/trade-marks-and-designs-if-theres-no-brexit-deal/trade-marks-and-designs-if-theres-no-brexit-deal

>> **Patents if there's no Brexit deal:** www.gov.uk/government/publications/patents-if-theres-no-brexit-deal

Looking at the bigger-picture intellectual property issues

If the UK leaves the EU under the terms of an agreed-upon withdrawal deal, with a transition period (see Chapter 3), then the UK government has said it will continue to protect all existing registered EU trademarks, registered community designs, and unregistered community designs after the UK exits the EU.

REMEMBER

For the duration of the transition period, EU law will continue to apply in the UK, so EU law relating to IP would still be relevant . . . for now.

In the longer term, beyond any transition period, both the UK and the EU have said they intend to maintain "current high levels of protection" for IP, as set out in the political declaration on future UK–EU negotiations (see Chapter 4). This indicates that the two parties will work together to explore IP options and cooperate to protect IP.

And what if the UK ends up leaving under a no-deal scenario? If the UK exits the EU without agreeing on a withdrawal deal, the government has still pledged to protect existing EU trademarks, registered community designs, and unregistered community designs.

The government has also said it'll preserve EU law on patents, copyright, and exhaustion of IP rights in the event of a no-deal Brexit, but that the UK might make "minor amendments and technical fixes in UK legislation as regards the preserved EU law, to ensure we have a functioning statute book after we leave the EU." Check out the links in the previous section to stay up to date on the latest deal-or-no-deal shenanigans and how they affect IP.

Taking action to protect your intellectual property

Whether the UK leaves the EU with a withdrawal deal or not, at some point, it's safe to assume that the protection afforded to UK intellectual property as a member of the EU might end.

REMEMBER

Broadly speaking, when the government says it'll continue to preserve IP rights, it means it'll set up comparable UK rights that mirror existing EU rights. This may mean that you need to register, say, your EU trademark in the UK to ensure continued protection in the UK as well as in the EU.

In other words, you may have to "roll over" your existing EU rights to cover the UK as well, but the timetable for doing this will depend on whether the UK exits with a deal and a transition period, or no deal. Again, check out the IP links earlier in the chapter to stay up to date on these plans.

REMEMBER

The situation for patents is less complicated because European-registered patents are governed by the European Patent Office, which is a non-EU agency that already accommodates non-EU members like Turkey and Norway. In other words, patents should be unaffected by Brexit.

There is, however, a new EU system in the works called the *Unitary Patent System,* which was expected to go live in 2017 but has been delayed because of — you guessed it — Brexit. This is a system for patent protection that will be valid in all participating EU member states. As of this writing, there have been proposals to include the UK in the Unitary Patent System after Brexit, although in the event of a no-deal scenario, this may change.

Continuing to Comply with Environmental Standards

The UK's environmental standards cover areas like waste, water, air quality, and the protection of habitats and species.

Pointing out that 80 percent of the UK's environmental standards come from the EU, organizations like Friends of the Earth have been quick to raise concerns that the UK government would use Brexit to reduce environmental standards and slash investment in environmental protections. The government, however, has said that it intends to honor environmental protection standards and uphold the UK's international agreements to protect or improve the environment.

REMEMBER

However Brexit plays out, the UK government has said that it's committed to maintaining environmental standards after the UK leaves the EU. Theresa May's withdrawal agreement (see Chapter 3), for example, ensures that EU environmental law continues to operate in UK law. And even if the UK leaves with no deal, the UK government has published guidance setting out how it intends to uphold environmental standards in the event of a no-deal Brexit.

To cement its commitment to the environment, the government has laid out a series of measures, including the following:

>> **A 25-year environment plan to improve the environment within a generation, entitled "A Green Future":** This includes talk of a "Green Brexit" (their words, not mine) that puts an emphasis on farming and agricultural policy.

>> **A new Environment Principles and Governance Bill:** The government says this bill will build on the 25-year environment plan and will ensure that environmental protections are not weakened after the UK leaves the EU.

>> **A new, independent statutory body to hold the government (current and future governments) to account over their environmental obligations.**

TIP

Read more about environmental standards and the impact of Brexit on the following web pages:

>> **25-Year Environment Plan:** www.gov.uk/government/publications/25-year-environment-plan

>> **New environment law to deliver a Green Brexit:** www.gov.uk/government/news/new-environment-law-to-deliver-a-green-brexit

>> **Upholding environmental standards if there's no Brexit deal:** www.gov.uk/government/publications/upholding-environmental-standards-if-theres-no-brexit-deal/upholding-environmental-standards-if-theres-no-brexit-deal

Maintaining Product Safety Standards

The UK government is under enormous pressure to ensure that current EU product safety standards are maintained after Brexit. So, although Brexit has been used by many as an argument to suggest that UK authorities may reduce product and consumer protections, this is unlikely to happen.

Looking at the big picture for safety standards

Setting aside the pressure from industry and consumers to maintain the UK's current high safety standards, there's also the subject of trading with the EU after Brexit.

REMEMBER

If the UK wants to agree on a close trading relationship with the EU, then it's most likely it will need to agree on broadly similar rules, regulations, and safety standards.

In fact, part of any trade agreement with other countries around the world (not just the EU) will likely involve safety standards and consumer protection promises. Leaving the EU and then converting the UK to a lower safety standard/consumer protection landscape wouldn't make much sense from an international trade perspective.

The problem comes if the UK finds itself under pressure to accept lower-standard goods from other countries as part of future trade negotiations. The often-quoted example of this is chlorine-washed chicken from the United States (a practice that's currently outlawed under EU and, in turn, UK laws). If, for example, the UK accepted products that don't meet European safety standards, then that may impact the UK's ability to negotiate a trade deal with the EU as part of its post-Brexit relationship.

Read more about trade in Chapter 5 and circle back to Chapter 4 to read more about the longer-term UK–EU relationship.

Considering the CE safety stamp on products

In the UK and Europe, many products (such as children's toys, household appliances, and even elevators) are marked with a safety stamp known as the *CE mark*.

This safety stamp shows consumers that the product they're buying or using meets EU safety requirements and has undergone safety tests.

REMEMBER

However, the CE mark is an EU safety marking, which means that after Brexit, UK products will need to have a new marking. This new symbol will be called *UKCA*, which stands for *UK Conformity Assessed.* The timeline for implementing this new stamp remains unclear at the time of this writing.

In the event that the UK leaves the EU with an approved withdrawal agreement, then nothing will change for the duration of any transition period — UK companies can continue to use the CE marking during the transition phase and will have plenty of time to prepare for the new UKCA marking.

In the event of a no-deal exit, however, the picture is much murkier. According to government advice published in February 2019, UK companies will continue to use the CE marking for products being sold in the UK for a "time-limited period unless your product requires third-party conformity assessment and if this has been carried out by a UK 'notified body.'" In these cases, you will instead have to apply for the new UKCA marking immediately after the UK leaves the EU.

The government has said that rules for the new UKCA marking will mirror those for the CE marking — meaning, if your product is currently covered by the CE marking, it should fall under the scope of the new UKCA stamp (medical devices are the one exception to this).

REMEMBER

However, the UKCA marking won't be recognized as a safety stamp on the EU market. So, if you sell any products in the EU that currently need a CE marking, you'll still need a CE marking if you want to continue selling those products in the EU.

TIP

Read more about the CE and UKCA markings here:

>> **Prepare to use the UKCA mark after Brexit:** www.gov.uk/government/publications/prepare-to-use-the-ukca-mark-after-brexit

>> **Using the UKCA marking if the UK leaves the EU without a deal:** www.gov.uk/government/publications/prepare-to-use-the-ukca-mark-after-brexit/using-the-ukca-marking-if-the-uk-leaves-the-eu-without-a-deal

>> **CE Marking Association:** www.cemarkingassociation.co.uk

Keeping Up with Other Legal and Regulatory Changes

Those in favor of Brexit often portray the legal workings of the EU as a case of the EU setting laws and the UK having to adopt those rules with no say in the matter.

But if you take a big step back and look at the situation from a distance, it's clear that, over the years, the UK government has been heavily involved in the creation of the EU legal and regulatory protections we all know and love (well, maybe not "know and love," depending on which side of the Brexit fence you fall).

While the UK is a member of the EU, these European rules are written into UK law. Going forward after Brexit, the UK government will have the option to transfer, amend, or remove these obligations that result from EU rules.

REMEMBER

In reality, we're unlikely to see any major amendments to UK legislation in the short and medium term. And even for the longer term, UK businesses and public bodies will continue to be bound by laws that are, most likely, broadly in line with EU regulations (although the UK will no longer have a say in what those EU regulations are, after it leaves the EU). If the UK and the EU want to maintain a close working relationship going forward (and both sides have so far said that's what they want — see Chapter 4), then it's unlikely we'll see major legal divergences.

That's because a close working relationship (not to mention any free-trade agreement that's negotiated) between the UK and the EU would probably require a similar legal and regulatory framework. There may be some tweaks and changes here and there, such as the need to re-register trademarks (as mentioned earlier in this chapter), but the UK way of life has been based upon EU laws for many years now — and that's unlikely to change in a big way.

That said, one interesting area to watch is employment law, because the UK government has indicated it may want to diverge from key EU employment protections such as the 48-hour workweek. (Indeed, the UK already allows workers to "opt out" of the 48-hour limit if they want to, but it may look to abolish the limit altogether.)

Time will tell if we do see some erosion of workers' rights after Brexit — after all, such plans would face serious opposition from the Labour Party and trade unions — but it's an interesting area where we may see some divergence between the UK and the EU. Head back to Chapter 7 to read more about the impact of Brexit on employment law and employing EU citizens after Brexit.

Always talk to your legal advisers about any changes in UK laws that occur after Brexit, to determine how your business may be affected.

What to Do If You Have a .eu Domain Name for Your Company Website

There are around 300,000 .eu domain names registered in the UK. If your company website is one of them, you'll need to prepare for changes that'll come into effect after Brexit.

The EU confirmed in March 2018 that .eu domain names will no longer be available to parties registered in the UK (including Gibraltar) after the UK exits the EU. This means UK organizations and individuals will be banned from acquiring domains ending in .eu as soon as the UK leaves the EU. What's more, the EU will have the right to revoke their existing .eu domains that are already registered to UK entities.

Does this mean your .eu domain name will be taken away from you? Quite possibly (although there is a way around this, which I'll get to later). We've yet to see how strict the EU will be in practice, but we should assume they mean business. So, working on the assumption that it's better to be safe than sorry, the question to ask isn't *if* your domain could be taken away, but *when.* . . .

If the UK exits the EU under the terms of a withdrawal agreement, it will enter a transition period, and the EU will not enforce its decision until the end of the transition period. However, if the UK exits the EU without a deal (hence, no transition period), then, in theory, the EU could reclaim .eu domain names immediately.

This is a perfectly legal and legitimate move on the part of the EU (because the EU regulatory framework for the .eu domain names simply won't apply to the UK after the UK leaves the EU). But there's no doubt it could cause a major headache for the hundreds of thousands of UK-based entities that already have .eu domains.

To help organizations get around this, many website hosting companies are now offering *proxy services.* Such proxy service providers will use a European subsidiary as the registration address for .eu domain names — meaning the legally registered owner and address for your .eu domain would be in Europe — and then lease the domain back to you so that you can continue to operate your website.

TIP

Using a proxy service for your .eu domain is a legal and legitimate way to protect your existing .eu domain. Check out proxy services from providers like www.hosting.co.uk for more information.

GDPR and Managing the Personal Data of EU Citizens

Unless you've been living under a rock for the past couple of years, you'll have read and heard a lot about the impact of the EU General Data Protection Regulation (GDPR), which came into force on May 25, 2018. But with GDPR being an EU regulation, will UK businesses still have to comply with GDPR rules after Brexit?

REMEMBER

The short answer is yes, businesses in the UK will still have to comply with GDPR rules even after Brexit. But, in some cases, the specifics of how your company handles data may change slightly after Brexit.

Recognizing that GDPR is enshrined in UK law

In a nutshell, GDPR is designed to give every EU citizen greater control over his or her personal data, including name, date of birth, and email address. It ensures that companies can't store and use the personal data of EU citizens without their explicit consent, and promotes the fair, transparent use of personal data.

REMEMBER

The fact that UK citizens will no longer be EU citizens after Brexit doesn't matter. Implementation of GDPR in the UK is covered by the UK Parliament's Data Protection Act 2018. So, GDPR is already written into UK law, and the government has committed to maintaining GDPR compliance in the UK. This ensures that UK citizens will continue to get all the same protections as their EU neighbors, when it comes to the fair use of their data.

This means all the protocols you've put in place to lawfully handle the data of your customers (whether they're in Europe or the UK) will still apply, and you should absolutely maintain compliance with GDPR.

But why continue with something that originated as EU law when so much of the rhetoric surrounding Brexit was about "taking back control"? The cynical answer is that businesses and public bodies in the UK have already spent millions ensuring their data practices were fully compliant with GDPR. If the government backtracked on GDPR now, it would mean all that expenditure was pointless. After all the time, effort, and money spent, it would be crazy to "undo" GDPR in the UK.

The less cynical answer is that GDPR is a good thing, for organizations and for individuals. Sure, it brings additional burdens in terms of compliance, but there's no doubt it provides important protections for citizens' private data. As technology advances and the world becomes increasingly driven by data, these protections will only become more valuable.

It's also important to remember that any close relationship between the UK and the EU going forward is likely to be dependent upon both parties having similar regulatory systems. Therefore, GDPR is just one area where British businesses will effectively be operating in line with European businesses.

Transferring data between the UK and the EU

Broadly speaking, how UK businesses handle personal data will stay the same. But there's a big uncertainty around what happens to businesses that transfer data between the UK and the remaining EU27 countries after Brexit (for example, if a company has offices in the UK and Europe, or if a UK business uses a cloud service provider based in the EU).

REMEMBER

Under GDPR, data cannot be transferred between the EU and *third countries* (non-EU countries) unless those countries have been deemed to have "adequate" data protections in place.

In the less likely event of a no-deal Brexit, the UK will immediately be considered a third country, which means that the European Commission will need to assess that the UK has adequate levels of protection in order for the smooth transfer of data to continue. (In theory, the Data Protection Act ensures that the UK does provide an adequate level of protection, but as with so much of Brexit, it's a case of wait and see whether this plays out in reality.)

And if the UK does exit with a withdrawal agreement in place, then, for the duration of any transition period, data transfers can continue as normal.

TIP

Stay up to date on the latest GDPR advice by visiting the following sites:

>> **Amendments to UK data protection law in the event the UK leaves the EU without a deal:** www.gov.uk/government/publications/data-

```
protection-law-eu-exit/amendments-to-uk-data-protection-
law-in-the-event-the-uk-leaves-the-eu-without-a-deal-on-
29-march-2019
```

» **International data transfers:** `https://ico.org.uk/for-organisations/`
`data-protection-and-brexit/data-protection-if-there-s-no-brexit-`
`deal/the-gdpr/international-data-transfers`

Reviewing Your Business Contracts

In addition to the other considerations set out in this chapter, you may also have to review your business contracts in light of Brexit.

WARNING

You may also need to renegotiate certain terms with suppliers and clients to mitigate the impact of currency fluctuations, changing costs relating to importing and exporting goods, and potentially longer lead times. Always work with a legal adviser before making any changes to contracts.

Generally speaking, if you own a UK business and you're reviewing your existing contracts, the following list serves as a good starting point. However, you should always discuss these and any other contractual changes with your legal adviser:

» From a big picture perspective, if your contract wording assumes that the UK is part of the EU (perhaps by referencing specific EU laws or obligations), this will need to be updated.

» If a contract references specific English laws (or the laws of another country within the UK), be prepared to update this in line with any legal amendments made after Brexit.

» If a contract states that it is subject to EU law, this might need to be updated to reflect that contracts will be covered by domestic law after Brexit.

» If the contract is challenged, you should clarify whether it would be challenged in a UK court or EU court.

» Pricing and delivery clauses may need updating in line with fluctuations or developments after Brexit.

TIP

It's a good idea to try to Brexit-proof your contracts as much as possible, by anticipating potential Brexit-related issues and uncertainties (such as supply chain delays; see Chapter 6) and limiting your contractual exposure to these issues.

You may also need to update your employment contracts to reflect any changes in employment law after Brexit. Circle back to Chapter 7 for more on potential changes to employment law after Brexit, and always talk to an employment law specialist to understand the full implications of any changes for your business.

IN THIS CHAPTER

» Looking at the implications for your workforce

» Assessing the impact on your trade and logistics

» Eyeing the money side of things

» Being prepared for changes in standards and licensing

» Considering the impact on your IT and data practices

» Accessing helpful tools to guide your contingency plan

Chapter **9**

Carrying Out a Brexit Impact Assessment for Your Business

S urely everyone knows the Boy Scouts motto of "Be prepared." I was a scout myself, and although I may have outgrown the desire to competitively cover my sash in merit badges (well, just about), the old "Be prepared" mind-set has always stayed with me.

Those scouts know what they're talking about. Whether you find yourself lost on a camping trip, or lost in the mad labyrinth of Brexit complexities, it's always a good idea to be prepared. You don't want to find yourself up Brexit Creek without a paddle.

And so I turn to the idea of conducting a Brexit impact assessment. Whatever industry your business operates in, it's a good idea to be prepared for whatever may come your way after Brexit. This involves asking yourself key questions on how Brexit may impact your company, so that you can plan for changes and revise your existing practices where necessary.

The lists of questions in this chapter are by no means exhaustive, and you'll undoubtedly need expert help in some areas to identify and plan for the full extent of changes after Brexit. I hope this chapter serves as a useful starting point — a basic framework to help you get the expert help you need, when you need it.

Assessing the Impact on Your Workforce

You can read more about employment-related issues in Chapter 7. In this section, I walk you through some of the key questions around your employees and access to labor. As you work through these questions, circle back to Chapter 7 for more information as and when you need it.

Employing EU nationals in the UK

When it comes to employing European Union (EU) citizens, consider the following:

» Do you employ any EU citizens in the United Kingdom (UK)?

» Do you plan to employ EU citizens in the UK in the future?

» Will your EU national employees remain in the UK after Brexit? Have you discussed their plans with them?

» Does your business rely on critical, skilled team members who are from the EU, and if so, how would the business cope without them?

» Have you informed your EU employees of their right to remain in the UK after Brexit?

» Are you giving your EU national employees the support and reassurance they may need at this uncertain time?

» Are your EU employees aware of the registration process for gaining *settled status* in the UK (see Chapter 7)?

» Is your workforce prepared for a no-deal Brexit? If there's no transition period, the timeline for registering for settled status may be impacted.

>> If your EU national employees choose to return to Europe, do you have the potential to recruit replacements easily?

>> Have you checked out the government's EU settlement scheme toolkit for employers? Find it at www.gov.uk/government/publications/eu-settlement-scheme-employer-toolkit.

TIP

Confusion and misunderstandings can be costly in terms of employee satisfaction and retention. Always keep your employees in the loop on Brexit developments and resulting changes in the business.

Maintaining access to labor

Depending on your business and industry, you may have some concerns about maintaining ongoing access to workers from the EU after Brexit. Read on for key questions to ask yourself at this time, and remember to circle back to Chapter 7 for more information.

>> Is there sufficient labor available in the local domestic market to replace EU national employees returning to their home countries?

>> How will you stay up to date on the latest UK government immigration plans and rules post-Brexit?

>> Under the government's immigration plans, unskilled workers from the EU will have the right to work in the UK for 12 months without getting a visa. Can you take advantage of this scheme to fill short-term and seasonal vacancies?

>> After Brexit, skilled workers from the EU will no longer have easier access to the UK jobs market than skilled workers from elsewhere in the world, and they may have to earn a minimum salary (which has been suggested at £30,000). Are you aware of immigration rules for recruiting skilled workers after Brexit?

>> Will it be harder and more costly to recruit in your industry after Brexit?

>> Have you planned for the potential impact on employment costs post-Brexit?

>> Will you have to offer higher salaries to recruit EU workers, if vacancies can't be filled by UK nationals?

>> If the company is planning to expand, have you considered your future workforce requirements and where you might be able to find suitable candidates?

Sending UK citizen employees to the EU

Your UK–national employees may need to travel to Europe on business. If so, consider the following:

>> Do any of your UK-based staff need to travel in the EU on business?

>> Have you considered changes in travel plans after Brexit?

>> Are you aware of the plans for short-term, visa-free travel in the EU after Brexit?

>> UK citizens looking to drive in Europe may need an international driving permit and insurance Green Card (especially in the event of a no-deal Brexit). Are your employees aware of this?

>> Do you have sufficient health insurance for UK employees traveling in Europe?

>> Do you have sufficient travel insurance (including air travel) for travel between the UK and EU?

>> Does each of your UK citizen employees traveling to Europe have a passport that's valid for at least six months after his or her stay?

>> If you have UK citizen employees based in Europe for the longer-term, will they need to re-register for residency in the country in which they're working?

>> How might any employee rights for UK citizens based in the EU be affected by a no-deal Brexit?

>> Have you considered taking on EU employees for EU-based roles, rather than sending UK employees to Europe, to ensure ease of movement across the EU?

>> If you have an EU-based subsidiary company or branch, will you continue to maintain that presence after Brexit? Is it cheaper and easier to outsource operations to a third-party provider in Europe instead of maintaining your own European presence?

Other employment-related issues

Here are some other employment–related questions you may want to consider:

>> How will you stay up to date on any changes in employment law after Brexit?

>> Do your employment contracts need updating in line with legal changes post-Brexit? (Read more about contracts in general in Chapter 8.)

» Even UK-born employees may be concerned about their jobs in light of Brexit. Are you communicating with *all* your employees about changes in the company and how employees may be affected?

» How will you manage any disruption, low morale, and problematic behavior that may arise amidst Brexit uncertainty?

» Employees crave greater recognition in times of business change or uncertainty. Are you giving your employees the recognition and reassurance they deserve?

» Do your employees have a forum in which to ask their Brexit-related questions?

» Does the company have a clear anti-discrimination policy, and are you prepared to nip any workforce friction in the bud?

» Are you closely monitoring employee engagement?

Considering the Impact on Trade and Logistics

Trading across borders (see Chapter 5) and logistics challenges (see Chapter 6) are two major considerations for businesses. In this section, I fill you in on some of the key questions your business should be asking to prepare for any potential impact.

General trade barriers and opportunities

What sort of trade barriers might your company face after Brexit? The following questions will help you assess the potential impact. You can find more information on trade barriers and trade agreements in Chapter 5.

» Will you still be able to trade your goods within Europe after Brexit?

» Have you considered the fact that some of your EU customers may seek EU-based companies to provide goods or services going forward?

» Is your particular industry likely to face much stricter checks on products coming and going between the UK and EU?

- » If new tariffs come into force, how will they affect your business?

- » Will your products still be competitively priced if new tariffs come into force?

- » Will changing tariff structures make it more attractive to import goods from non-EU markets?

- » Are you aware of the relevant EU product classifications for tariffs?

- » If you provide services to EU customers, will you have to get authorization from the country in which you're operating to continue providing that service?

- » Will barriers to trade between the UK and EU open up new markets within the UK for your business? For example, will more UK consumers in your sector be looking for homegrown solutions?

- » How will you stay up to date on trade negotiations between the UK and EU, and the potential impact on your business?

Importing and exporting goods

If you import or export goods to or from the EU, you may want to consider the following sorts of questions. Head back to Chapter 5 to read more about the potential impact of Brexit on importing and exporting.

- » Does your business import or export goods to or from the EU?

- » If so, are you aware of the potential changes in procedures regarding importing and exporting between the UK and the EU?

- » Are you aware of any additional paperwork needed for goods that are being imported and exported?

- » Have you considered employing specialist staff, or partnering with a third party, to help with import/export documentation and changing procedures?

- » Is there scope to open an office in the EU or partner with an EU provider to assist with importing and exporting?

- » Can your current software packages cope with changes in importing/exporting procedures and paperwork?

- » Are you up to date on the government's latest plans for the new Customs Declaration System for UK importers and exporters (see Chapter 6)?

- » Do your employees have the information they need to carry out their import- and export-related duties correctly?

- >> Do you need to get proof of origin on components and products coming from the EU in order to complete your paper trail?

- >> Have you factored in the inevitable increase in importing and exporting costs going forward?

- >> Are you prepared for potential changes in value-added tax (VAT) payments and customs duties on imports from the EU?

- >> Have you considered working with a customs broker and/or customs warehouse provider?

- >> Is there scope to build any new tariffs into your current pricing structure?

- >> How will you stay up to date on the latest importing and exporting rules and procedures?

- >> Are you looking into potential new markets and suppliers beyond the EU, and assessing their individual import and export procedures?

Potential supply chain disruption

Any changes to import and export procedures, as outlined in the previous sections, may result in some disruption to your supply chain. Ask yourself the following impact assessment questions, and return to Chapter 6 for more information on potential supply chain and logistics impacts.

- >> Is any part of your supply chain dependent upon goods coming from the EU? (**Remember:** This will involve your suppliers and where *they* source their goods from.)

- >> Do you or any of your suppliers store goods in an EU-based warehouse? (Even if your goods originate from outside the EU, they may still temporarily be held in an EU warehouse.)

- >> Are you aware of the need for commercial trailers to be registered with the Driver and Vehicle Licensing Agency (DVLA) before traveling abroad?

- >> Are your drivers or transportation providers aware of the documents they need to carry for driving in Europe after Brexit?

- >> Have you considered potential time and cost implications of supply chain disruption?

- >> What is your contingency plan if goods are delayed exiting or entering the UK or EU?

- » How will you manage customer or client expectations regarding short-term teething problems?

- » Will you need to adjust customer expectations with regards to delivery times?

- » How will you keep customers informed of post-Brexit changes?

- » Do any of your contracts include penalties for late delivery?

- » Do you need to update your standard terms and conditions to take account of supply chain changes?

- » Have you spoken with your suppliers about any potential supply chain issues they may face, and how this may affect the service they provide for you?

- » Are your suppliers making their own Brexit contingency plans? If they're not, this could affect your business.

- » Have you spoken with your transport/haulage providers about changes to procedures or timescales after Brexit?

- » Are your haulage providers already facing a driver shortage and, if so, do they expect this to get worse after Brexit?

- » Do you have a sufficient stockpile of components and stock to see you through any short-term teething problems, especially if there's a no-deal Brexit? If not, are you able to stockpile critical components or goods? Can you afford to?

- » Is your warehousing provider operating at capacity because of other companies stockpiling goods? Do you need to look for alternative or overflow warehousing space?

- » Are your logistics suppliers planning to raise their prices in light of Brexit?

- » Can you avoid supply chain delays by switching to other suppliers outside of the EU (either in the UK or further afield)?

- » How might technology solutions help to mitigate supply chain disruption and make your supply chain more efficient in the future?

Looking at the Money Side of Things

Pretty much all the considerations laid out in this chapter and throughout the rest of the chapters in Part 3 may have an impact on your bottom line. Therefore, for each consideration so far, you'll need to think about how Brexit-related changes may affect your company's revenue, costs, and cash flow.

Here are some key financial questions to kickstart your preparations.

VAT, accounting, costs, and cash flow

As with any business change, you'll no doubt want to discuss the impact of Brexit with your accountant and/or financial adviser. The following questions should serve as a good starting point for those discussions.

» Have you spoken with your accountant regarding potential cash flow issues?

» Do you have additional funding available to offset potential cash flow issues?

» Have you made plans to boost your profitability and reduce costs wherever possible?

» Are you able to extend payment terms with suppliers to mitigate cash flow issues?

» Is it possible to reduce the period of time between taking ownership of imported goods and receiving funds from the sale of those goods?

» Does your company hold money in EU institutions or regularly move money between the UK and the EU?

» The transfer of funds between the UK and the EU may need to be reported in a different way going forward. How will you stay abreast of changing obligations?

» Is your business VAT registered and how will you be affected by any changes in VAT rules?

» How will VAT or customs duties on imports impact your cash flow?

» Have you planned for a worst-case scenario regarding VAT and customs duties?

» Is there potential to offset potential VAT issues and customs duty increases with efficiency improvements in the business?

» Are there any other implications for your business in terms of accounting practices (such as double taxation rules)?

» Have you factored in the cost of seeking expert advice where needed? (See Chapter 10 for more on building a dream team of advisers.)

» Are there any business processes that you could automate or outsource to reduce costs? (See Chapter 11 for more business opportunities to take advantage of at this time.)

TIP

Talk to your accountant about potential cash flow issues in the wake of Brexit.

Grants and funding

Many businesses that benefit from government funding are concerned that Brexit may limit their access to funding in the future. Read on if this applies to your business.

>> Is your business reliant on funding or grants that come from the EU? (This may include UK government grants that were backed by the EU.)

>> If so, does the UK government plan to introduce similar grants and funding to replace those previously provided by the EU?

>> Are there any new or existing domestic grants or funding programs you can apply for?

>> Will your business still be viable if EU funding is removed and not replaced by the UK government?

>> Is there a case for moving your operations to the EU to take advantage of EU grants and funding in the future?

Currency issues

Depending on your business model (for example, if you export goods to Europe), the weaker pound may bring positive business benefits. But how else might currency fluctuations impact your business? Read on to find out.

>> Have you considered currency exchange issues?

>> How will you monitor currency exchange issues going forward?

>> Have you made plans for potentially offsetting volatility in the future, perhaps by hedging or negotiating a fixed sterling rate with EU suppliers?

>> If your goods are more competitive and attractive to overseas customers as a result of the weaker pound, are you capitalizing on this? How can you increase your sales while the pound remains weak? (For more Brexit-related business opportunities, turn to Chapter 11.)

Bringing Standards, Licensing, and Qualifications Up to Date

In this section, I walk you through some of the issues around professional and product standards. You can read more about standards in Chapter 8.

Professional qualifications and licensing

When it comes to professional qualifications, you may need to ask yourself the following sorts of questions:

>> Will current UK professional qualifications or licenses be recognized in the EU going forward?

>> Will those in the business need to seek EU qualifications to complement their UK ones?

>> If any of your employees are moving between UK and EU subsidiaries, will they require additional qualifications or licensing?

Operating and product standards

UK businesses are used to operating in line with EU standards. But how might that change after Brexit? Check out the questions in this section. and read more about product and safety standards in Chapter 8.

>> Does your company produce goods that must adhere to EU standards?

>> Are any of your operations governed by EU standards?

>> Are you aware of changes to UK standards in light of Brexit?

>> Will your ongoing product safety standards be comparable with EU standards (essential for exporting to the EU)?

>> Have you considered extra paperwork or certification that may be required to prove comparable safety standards?

>> Do all the components you use in your products satisfy EU safety standards?

>> Can you provide proof of origin for your products or components if needed?

Environmental standards

The UK government has committed to maintaining environmental protections, so little is expected to change for UK businesses in this regard. However, you may want to consider the following questions and circle back to Chapter 8 for more information on environmental standards:

>> Are you aware of the government's continuing commitment to environmental standards?

>> Will you be abiding by EU recycling/waste regulations going forward?

Assessing IT and Data Implications

Here are the questions you should be asking to assess the impact of Brexit on your IT and data practices:

» Have you reinforced the importance of continuing to comply with the EU General Data Protection Regulation (GDPR) after Brexit?

» Do you transfer data between the UK and EU, or is your data hosted in an EU country (for example, by a cloud storage provider)?

» After Brexit, as a *third country* (a non-EU country), the UK will have to prove it meets acceptable data standards to transfer data between the UK and the EU. Are your systems able to provide the information that may be needed going forward?

» Have you looked at the Information Commissioner's Office tool for guidance on GDPR and data protection after Brexit? Find it at `https://ico.org.uk/ for-organisations/data-protection-and-brexit/data-protection- if-there-s-no-brexit-deal`.

» How will you stay up to date on the latest GDPR-related information?

» Do you need to update your website information, including terms and conditions and delivery information/costs?

» If you have an `.eu` domain name for your website, have you made plans to retain your domain after Brexit through a proxy hosting service?

» Do your employees traveling in Europe have sufficient mobile phone coverage in terms of data and calls?

You can read more about GDPR and website changes in Chapter 8.

Covering Miscellaneous Considerations

Finally, I want to look at all the niggly items that don't fit neatly under the previous headings. Many of these subjects are covered in more detail in Chapter 8.

>> Will Brexit affect your company structure in any way? This is particularly relevant if you have overseas subsidiary businesses.

>> Do you need to change your company registration at Companies House?

>> Is it worth establishing formal relationships with EU-based companies to eliminate your own need to have a subsidiary business in the EU?

>> Are there any opportunities to expand your business by acquiring subsidiaries of EU-based companies that no longer want to operate in the UK?

>> Have you taken precautions to protect your copyright, brand names, logos, patents, and other intellectual property?

>> Is your UK-based insurance still valid within the EU post-Brexit?

>> Have you made plans to revise your contracts where necessary, including where they refer to EU law?

>> How will legal disputes be resolved post-Brexit?

>> Have you reviewed the potential regulatory changes that may impact your business?

>> Do you need to update your internal policies and procedures?

>> Are you in touch with your trade association for general advice?

>> Have you signed up for government alerts on Brexit? You can sign up at `www.gov.uk/government/brexit`.

Making Sure You Have a Contingency Plan

Contingency planning is all about making sure your business can cope with the changes or disruptions that may come your way after Brexit, whether these are short-term blips or long-term changes.

The questions I outline in this chapter will help you prepare your business for any potential Brexit outcomes. But remember, these questions are just a starting point. You may well need expert help to prepare detailed contingency plans or assess industry-specific implications for your business.

TIP

To help get your business in good shape for Brexit, I highly recommend the following tools:

» **Business Brexit Checklist from the British Chambers of Commerce:** www.britishchambers.org.uk/media/get/Business%20Brexit%20Checklist.pdf

» **Official government tool to help businesses prepare for Brexit:** www.gov.uk/business-uk-leaving-eu

Turn to Part 4, where I set out more tips for business owners and leaders, including how to protect your business against Brexit uncertainty, what sort of opportunities may lie ahead for British businesses after Brexit, and key Brexit developments to keep an eye on.

The Part of Tens

IN THIS PART . . .

Maintain a successful business during political and economic uncertainty.

Identify new business opportunities that result from Brexit.

Stay in the loop on the latest Brexit developments and unresolved issues.

Chapter **10**

Ten (Or So) Ways to Protect Your Business against Brexit Uncertainty

B rexit, market shifts, global financial crises, advancing technology — businesses have always had to cope with uncertainty and change in one way or another.

REMEMBER

When the going gets tough — whether it's temporary disruption or huge industry change — the businesses that survive (and thrive, in fact) are the ones that keep their eyes on the ball while finding ways to adapt.

This chapter looks at practical ways to maintain a successful business, even when times are changing and uncertainty is rife. Whether you're a small business owner, a leader in a larger company, or the manager of a team, this chapter helps you keep focused, stay positive, and continue to deliver great results.

And if you're interested in capitalizing on exciting commercial opportunities in the post-Brexit world, head to Chapter 11. There, you find a bunch of business growth ideas that could help you take your business to the next level.

Doing a Brexit Impact Assessment

There's an old saying in business: You can't manage what you don't measure. Sure, Peter Drucker, the management guru who coined the phrase, was talking about using key performance indicators to track progress, but I think there's a deeper lesson to learn here. Namely, if you don't first get the lay of the land, how on earth can you expect to steer your business or team in the right direction? If you don't understand the potential impact of Brexit, how can you manage it?

TIP

Therefore, if you happened to skip over Chapter 9, which is all about conducting a Brexit impact assessment, pause here. Circle back to that chapter to get a handle on the many sorts of questions your business should be asking at this time. These questions will help you to assess which parts of the business might be affected by Brexit, and plan an appropriate way forward.

Working with a "Dream Team" of Experts

As the owner of several businesses including www.propertyforum.com, I couldn't function without what I call my "dream team." (The dream team is a core element of my property investment book, *Investing in International Real Estate For Dummies*, which is also published by Wiley.)

My dream team comprises experts in all the fields where I lack specialized skills and knowledge, including accounting, tax, law, and so on. These are my professional advisers, and I rely on them to give me the most relevant, accurate, and up-to-date advice I need to steer my businesses correctly.

REMEMBER

Brexit is a complicated, evolving subject, and you'll undoubtedly need professional expertise to guide you in certain areas as the business climate changes. If you already have that expertise in house, great! Consider, though, whether your in-house dream team could benefit from upskilling and training to ensure they have all the right knowledge and tools at this time.

TIP

If you don't have the people in house, it's never too late to start expanding your network and connecting with expert, external services. This may involve:

>> Connecting with specialists via your local networking groups

>> Seeking word-of-mouth recommendations from people you know and trust

>> Connecting with experts online via LinkedIn and specialist forums

You could, of course, spend an awful lot of your own time keeping up with nitty-gritty Brexit developments, researching legal implications, deciphering potential tax changes, and all that jazz — but is that really the best approach for your business or the best use of your time? Probably not. (See "Keeping Your Foot on the Gas," later in this chapter.) That's what your professional advisers are for.

Besides, in my opinion, it's not a great idea to rely on your own reading of the Brexit situation. If you misread new rules, for instance, it could end up costing your business dearly in the long term. Seek professional advice and make sure your business gets it right the first time.

Staying in the Loop on Brexit Developments

Remember when I said not to get too embroiled in the latest, nitty-gritty Brexit developments? (Of course you do, it was only a couple of paragraphs ago.) To be clear, I wasn't giving you permission to ignore Brexit developments altogether, or bury your head in the sand. Sticking your fingers in your ears and singing "la la la" — tempting though it may be sometimes — isn't much of a strategy.

REMEMBER

Bottom line: You do still need to stay in the loop on the latest big-picture Brexit news. Even if the latest development isn't what you, personally, wanted to see happen. Even if you're exhausted by the subject (as many people are). If you don't stay up to date at a basic level, how will you know what questions to ask your dream team of expert advisers?

Turn to Chapter 12, and you'll find some helpful sources of Brexit information, and some of the (at the time of writing) as-yet unresolved issues to keep a close eye on.

Engaging with Government Support and Business Resources

Many business owners, leaders, and managers are in the same boat as you — trying to pick their way through an extremely complicated subject and unearth the practical implications for their business. You're not alone, in other words.

Recognizing this need for clear information, the government and lots of independent organizations are offering support for businesses. The Confederation of British Industry (www.cbi.org.uk) is one great example of this, and you can find other helpful resources in Chapter 12.

Keeping Your Foot On the Gas

In my experience, change usually affects a company in one of two ways:

>> **It spurs the business on to evolve and adapt.** In this scenario, change is a force for good, something that encourages innovation, positivity, and excitement.

>> **It sucks the energy and motivation from a business.** People get distracted by temporary uncertainty. Engagement dips. Negativity rises. Everyday business activity suffers.

Which camp do you want your business to be in?

Don't let your business get distracted by Brexit-related uncertainty (or any business uncertainty, for that matter). Don't get bogged down or take your foot off the gas.

REMEMBER

Stay focused on your core activities at this time — and by "core activities" I mean continuing to deliver outstanding products, and wowing your customers or clients with incredible service. I mean, isn't that why you started the business in the first place? (Or, if you're an employee, isn't that why you get out of bed and go to work each day?)

If you let that everyday activity slip, if you don't stay true to your business's mission, even if it's just for a little while, your customers will notice. Don't give them an excuse to take their business elsewhere. (See also "Communicating with Your Customers" later in the chapter.)

Diversifying and Creating Multiple Streams of Income

I mention in the last section that, during uncertain times, keeping your business doing what it does best is vital. There's a counterpoint to that important rule: While maintaining your core everyday business activity, you may also want to take this opportunity to consider diversifying your business and finding new sources of revenue.

REMEMBER

Any business that's reliant on one market, one big customer, one major supplier, or one single product is vulnerable. Over-reliance on one thing is risky at any time, but especially so in uncertain times — and especially when it comes to revenue. That's why, wherever possible, you should look for ways to grow your business through new revenue streams.

This may mean:

>> Developing new products and services

>> Expanding into new geographic regions

>> Targeting new customer segments

>> Partnering with or acquiring another provider who brings something new and exciting to the party

>> Expanding your professional network

I'm an eternal optimist, and I like to think that life after Brexit will offer plenty of fantastic business opportunities — for me and for you. With that in mind, I suggest some post-Brexit business opportunities in Chapter 11.

After the United Kingdom (UK) has exited the European Union (EU) — assuming the UK exits under the terms of a withdrawal agreement (see Chapter 3) — there's then a formal *transition period* that's likely to run until December 2020, but could run until December 2022, or later, depending on when the UK leaves. (Turn back to Chapter 1 for more about the transition period and Brexit timeline.) Think of this transition period as your innovation and diversification period. In other words, you've got X many months to a) think about where your company is going and how best to evolve and future-proof the business, and b) put those plans into action. Turn Brexit into an opportunity — that's the message!

Small businesses are at a big advantage here, because they can usually innovate, adapt, and respond to market changes quicker than huge multinational corporations, with their many layers of leadership and approval processes. If you're a small business, find a way to take advantage of the market conditions. Don't be afraid to experiment. Find out what works and what doesn't for your business, keep pushing and always be growing.

Working with a business adviser is a great way to identify and assess new business opportunities and find ways to grow your business. Look for a local business adviser or consultant wherever possible (perhaps through local networking groups or word-of-mouth recommendations). A local adviser can really get to know your business in depth, and the two of you can develop that important face-to-face rapport. Also, review your marketing efforts and don't join the masses and cut marketing spend through fear. One of my favorite mantras is: Observe the masses and do the opposite, and you won't go wrong. While your competition panics and loses market share through inaction, you can take this opportunity to get ahead!

Keeping Staff Engaged and Motivated

Some of your employees may be EU citizens unsure of their rights in the UK after Brexit. These employees will obviously need clear information and support from your business (more on this in Chapter 7).

But whether your employees hail from Spain, South America, or Southend-on-Sea, Brexit uncertainty has the potential to cause unease among the workforce. People may have big fears about the business as a whole or, on a smaller scale, be worried about certain processes or their roles changing.

Few things kill off staff engagement and motivation faster than uncertainty, so make sure to manage this carefully. For the most part, this is about communicating openly and clearly with staff on how the business will be impacted (if at all), where there may be changes, and how those changes will be managed.

In other words, reassure your employees that you're on top of the situation, and that there's a plan (or that a plan is being developed, which is better than nothing).

Above all, remind your employees of the business's mission and goals at this time, and the need for everyone to keep doing what they're doing — delivering awesome products and delighting customers with amazing service.

If you aren't already monitoring employee engagement on a regular basis, now may be a good time to start. Gone are the days of expensive, time-consuming annual staff surveys; these days, there are tons of inexpensive tools that can assess employee mood frequently, using just a few well-chosen questions.

Communicating with Your Customers

Just as you should be communicating openly with your employees during uncertain times, you also need to be communicating openly with your customers and suppliers (more on suppliers coming up next).

Your customers will need to know whether anything is likely to change after the UK is no longer part of the EU. For example, are overseas orders likely to take a few days longer? Are prices changing? Are you offering new products and services?

In short, keep communicating with your customers, and reassure them that it's business as usual in terms of your company delivering outstanding customer service.

Make sure your customer communications don't fall foul of General Data Protection Regulation (GDPR) rules. Flip back to Chapter 8 for more on GDPR and personal data.

Communicating with Your Suppliers

The impact of Brexit on your supply chain will depend on what type of business you run and the suppliers you work with. But, whatever the impact (if any), it's vital you maintain a clear line of communication with your suppliers.

Are your suppliers keeping you up to date on any potential service changes or delays? If not, press them for more information and ask them for more regular updates. After all, you've got to keep your own customers informed.

There may be times when the picture is a little foggy. A supplier may, for example, know that a particular process will change, but not yet have 100 percent certainty on *how* it will change. That's understandable. What you need is transparent communication on what's definitely happening, where there may be gray areas, and a timeline for resolving any unknowns.

If both parties can maintain that open line of communication, you'll be well placed to weather uncertainty together and emerge with a stronger, closer business relationship.

Chapter **11**

Ten (Or So) Business Opportunities for a Post-Brexit World

So much of the news around Brexit, and particularly the impact of Brexit on business, has been, well, not exactly cheerful. (Some would say downright doom and gloom, while others might say hysterical.) And although there are obviously issues to be aware of and prepare for — which is the whole idea behind Part 3 of this book — plenty of businesses are finding positive opportunities in the face of Brexit.

This chapter looks at just a few of the potential opportunities that businesses in the United Kingdom (UK) could exploit as a result of Brexit.

REMEMBER

Some of these are short-term opportunities, while others may take longer to pay off. And some will be more applicable to your company than others. I'm not offering one-size-fits-all solutions here. It's up to you to pick and choose the ideas that may deliver the most value for your business.

Pick one or two ideas from this chapter that you think best apply to your business, taking into account the size of your company, your capabilities, where your business is in its life cycle, and the wider industry in which you operate. Having cherry-picked the most applicable opportunities, you can then investigate them further.

Exploring New Markets Beyond the EU

If you're already exporting goods outside the UK, or you're eager to explore overseas markets, Brexit could deliver a welcome boost. Or, more specifically, the devalued pound resulting from Brexit uncertainty could help to boost your export sales.

A weaker pound tends to help companies that export goods overseas, because it makes UK products cheaper than those produced in countries with stronger currencies.

For a reverse illustration of this, consider imports of cheap Chinese steel. Even though the product is coming all the way from China, it may still be cheaper than British steel, because it costs a Chinese steel producer less to manufacturer than it costs a British company.

The UK's ability to negotiate trade deals with other countries is, at the time of writing, far from crystal clear. So, to fully understand the impact on your exports, stay tuned to future trade negotiations. (See Chapter 12 for the top Brexit developments to keep an eye on, including trade negotiations.)

Growing Domestic Demand for Products and Services

What's the flip side of cheaper UK exports being more attractive to overseas buyers? Imports from outside the UK become more expensive for UK businesses and consumers.

Of course, if you're importing parts or products from abroad, this will cause you some headaches in terms of profitability, in which case, you may be looking to trade more with UK partners. But, on the positive side, rising import prices can bring big benefits.

REMEMBER

When foreign products become more expensive (perhaps because of currency fluctuations or trade tariffs), consumers tend to look closer to home for goods and services. In other words, your business may be more competitive than foreign companies.

Capitalizing on Reduced Regulation

On the whole, the UK is likely to remain fairly closely aligned with European Union (EU) rules. Yet, in some areas, it's possible that post-Brexit changes to regulations and standards may offer UK businesses greater freedom and flexibility than EU rules.

REMEMBER

Reduced regulation may make your business processes easier and quicker, and potentially reduce your costs — all of which could make your business more competitive.

Read more about changing regulation and standards in Chapter 8.

Solving Your Customers' Brexit-Related Problems

If you've struggled to comprehend the implications of Brexit for your business, it's fair to assume that some or all of your customers (and potential customers) may find themselves in the same boat.

TIP

Consider whether there's a market opportunity to offer tailored Brexit services to your customers. Ask yourself, "What are our customers struggling with in relation to Brexit, and how can we help them to solve those problems?"

Now, I'm not suggesting you set up a new business as an all-singing-all-dancing Brexit consultancy service (although, for those who have the skills and knowledge, such a business would probably prove quite valuable in the short term). Instead, I'm talking about:

>> **Tailoring your products and services in line with your customers' Brexit "pain points."** These pain points could be around access to labor, VAT, cash flow, stockpiling goods, seeking investment, or whatever.

>> **Tweaking your marketing messages to emphasize how your business is ready to help clients overcome Brexit hurdles.**

For example, if you're an accountant primarily dealing with small and midsize firms, your clients may need extra support to understand potential VAT changes — in which case, you're there to guide them through changes and help them implement new processes.

Or, if you run a legal firm dealing with employment law, you're well placed to help local businesses that employ workers from outside the UK stay on the right side of the law.

If you're a business coach or adviser, your clients may be looking to explore new growth strategies for their company or revise their business strategy in light of Brexit developments.

REMEMBER

This strategy is a relatively short-term one, but you may find it pays long-term dividends. By positioning your business as more prepared and more thoughtful than your competitors, you have the opportunity to gain market share and raise your company's profile.

Building Your Personal Reputation as a Leader in Your Industry

In addition to raising the profile of your business, as suggested in "Solving Your Customers' Brexit-Related Problems," Brexit may also present a tantalizing career opportunity for you.

Where possible, collaborate with others outside your own organization to discuss Brexit implications, stay in the loop on the industry's response, and strengthen your personal network.

TIP

Here are just a few ways you could potentially increase your personal profile within your industry in light of Brexit:

» Engage on a broader scale outside your business by joining Brexit committees set up by your trade association or other organizations in your field.

» If the government asks for participation and consultation in your area of expertise, consider getting involved.

» Publish online articles and white papers setting out how your company is dealing with Brexit implications and staying ahead of the field.

>> If you work in a large organization, you could volunteer to represent the company on industry committees and working groups, or present updates to the company's leadership team on how your department is managing Brexit implications.

Automating Business Processes

Rising automation is a huge topic in business, thanks largely to massive leaps in technology, robotics, artificial intelligence and so on. If your company hasn't already looked at the potential to automate processes and roles, now is a good time to start.

Looking at automation opportunities is a bit like renewing your car insurance. We all know we shouldn't just stick with the status quo and accept the renewal price from our current insurer; we know that if we spent half a day calling around dozens of insurers, we could get a better deal elsewhere. Yet, when renewal time comes around, how many of us take the easy route and stick with the status quo? Come on, you're among friends, be honest. I know I've been guilty of this in the past!

Think of exploring automation as being forced to renew your car insurance the "proper" way. Sticking with the status quo isn't an option, not unless you've really done your homework and you're sure there isn't a better alternative out there.

REMEMBER

Automation may be particularly relevant if your business is reliant on labor from overseas to fulfill critical business functions. If attracting British workers isn't a realistic option (some industries do struggle to recruit locally and have to look farther afield), then automating certain processes may be an unavoidable long-term strategy for your business.

You may think automation only applies in manufacturing or agricultural contexts, but think again. A wide range of business processes are increasingly being automated, across all sorts of business functions, including HR, sales, marketing, and finance. For example, in sales, software can now automate lead prioritization, scheduling appointments, and logging follow-up tasks.

REMEMBER

Automation doesn't necessarily mean taking jobs away from human workers and giving them to machines. In a lot of cases, automation simply improves what human employees do by helping to streamline processes. And when your human employees are freed up from more menial, repetitive tasks (such as scheduling appointments), they have more time to focus on tasks that directly benefit the business.

Therefore, use Brexit as an excuse to review your processes across the business and see where you have an opportunity to automate and improve processes. As a big believer in work–life balance and the passive income mind-set, I'm constantly reviewing processes in my businesses to see what can be done quicker, cheaper, and easier with software or well-designed systems.

Seeking Investment from Overseas Investors

My primary line of work is in real estate investment and real estate development. From what I've seen, there's a definite sense that overseas investors have been holding back from investing in UK real estate development projects in light of Brexit uncertainty. In other words, there's potentially a massive backlog of external investment just waiting to pile into the UK property market after the dust settles, especially because the pound is weak and investments represent better value and yield.

My experience in the real estate sector is indicative of a wider downturn in foreign investment. Figures from the Organisation for Economic Co-operation and Development (OECD) show that foreign investment fell 90 percent in 2017, after a bumper 2016. That's obviously concerning in the short term, but the long-term picture is more positive, with many believing that foreign investment will flood back into the country after Brexit.

REMEMBER

Why would overseas investors want to invest in UK businesses and projects? Quite simply, because the weak pound means their money goes further in the UK. They get more bang for their buck (or euros, or whatever) and the UK fundamentally remains an excellent investment location. So, when the short-term uncertainty is over, I believe external investment will pick up the pace.

TIP

Investment promotion agencies may be able to help your business attract foreign investors. (InvestUK is one example of such an agency. Check them out at www. investuk.com.) You can also get help and advice from the Department for International Trade (www.gov.uk/government/organisations/department-for-international-trade).

Picking Up Business from Companies That Have Left the UK

In the event that a direct competitor pulls out of the UK, consider whether there's a chance to suck up some of their business. This could, for example, involve buying their client lists (where possible), advertising to their primary audience, or even acquiring the UK arm of an EU company.

Take the UK fishing industry as a big-picture example. If EU countries lose the right to fish in British waters after Brexit, this could give UK fleets a much fairer share of fishing rights. (In 2018, EU fleets were landing eight times as much fish in UK waters as British fleets were landing in EU waters.)

REMEMBER

Whether you're a fisherman or a financial adviser, if your competitors leave a gap to be filled, make sure your business is the one that fills it. Be ready to expand your market share and attract new customers.

Capitalizing on Homegrown Support for British Businesses

Many in the UK see Brexit as an opportunity to become more self-sufficient, to prioritize homegrown solutions over imported products and services. (In the case of the agricultural sector, the word *homegrown* is highly relevant because imported food potentially becomes more expensive.)

This isn't just about Brexit, though. For all sorts of reasons, including climate change, more and more people are thinking "local" rather than "global." Local producers, local suppliers, local services — all offer an opportunity for customers, clients, and consumers to feel more connected to the companies they deal with.

REMEMBER

People in the UK want to support UK businesses. If you're a local alternative to faceless, global entities, don't be afraid to say so!

Chapter **12**

Ten Brexit Developments to Keep an Eye On

B rexit is a complicated subject that's constantly evolving. Some issues are simply unresolved or unclear at the time of writing this book; others, such as trade, are subject to ongoing negotiations. Brexit is a bit like playing whack-a-mole in that sense — one uncertainty gets resolved or one hurdle is cleared (whack!), and another one pops up immediately to take its place.

REMEMBER

Therefore, you can't really consider the job of "understanding" Brexit and its implications done anytime soon. Even after the United Kingdom (UK) has left the European Union (EU), it may take years to fully realize some of the effects or implement certain legal and policy changes. That means you need to stay in the loop on the latest Brexit developments if you want to steer your business correctly.

In this chapter, I suggest key topics that you may want to keep an eye on (while steering clear of the obvious questions on everyone's lips, such as "When will Brexit happen?" or even "*Will* Brexit happen?"). Some topics, such as Scottish independence, have wider implications for the UK as a whole, while others, such as workforce pressures, may directly impact your business over time. (No doubt, you'll care more about some of these issues than others, and that's fine. As with the rest of the chapters in this book, focus on what's most relevant to you.) Finally, at the end of the chapter, I list some useful sources that will help you to stay up to date.

The Transition Period

The Brexit withdrawal deal allows for a transition period (see Chapter 3), where certain things, like trade arrangements and the UK abiding by EU rules, will continue unchanged until December 2020, or whenever the transition period is set to end.

REMEMBER

This transition period could potentially be extended until as late as December 2022 (perhaps even later), if the UK and the EU agree. If the transition period is extended, this will impact the Brexit timeline (see Chapter 1), because UK companies will still be bound by EU rules for the duration. This is either a good thing or a bad thing, depending on which side of the Brexit fence you fall.

Those in favor of extending the transition period say it'll give the UK more time to negotiate a trade deal with the EU. Most experts agree that December 2020 doesn't give nearly enough time to negotiate a trade deal. (As an example, Canada's trade agreement with the EU took seven years!)

Meanwhile, those against an extension are unhappy at the idea of being hitched to the EU for any longer than necessary. They'd much rather take a "rip off the Band-Aid" approach.

Trade Negotiations with the EU and Beyond

We don't yet know how the UK will trade with Europe and the rest of the world after it leaves the EU. What sort of barriers will there be to moving goods across borders? What tariffs will apply? The answer, for now, is anyone's guess.

REMEMBER

Obviously, if you import or export goods, this is an issue you'll be watching intensely, and you don't need me to tell you it's important! Instead, let me take this opportunity to highlight some of the options that have been proposed for the UK's future trade relationship with the EU:

>> **A Norway-style deal,** which would see the UK remain in the single market but leave the customs union (see Chapter 2 for an explanation of these terms). Upside? The UK would have full access to the single market with no barriers. Downside? The UK would have to accept freedom of movement and be subject to EU regulations (without having a say in setting those regulations, as EU members do).

>> **A Turkey-style deal,** in which the UK would leave the single market but remain in a customs union with the EU. Upside? Likely tariff-free trade between the UK and the EU. Downside? The UK would have to apply the EU's common external tariff on goods from non-EU countries, which might hamper the UK's trade negotiations with other countries.

>> **A Canada- or Switzerland-style deal**, whereby the UK leaves the single market and customs union but negotiates a tailor-made free trade agreement with the EU. This is the route Switzerland and Canada have taken. Upside? Likely tariff-free trade. Downside? The UK *may* have to comply with EU law and/or accept free movement of people, like Switzerland does.

>> **Trading under World Trade Organization (WTO) rules,** in which the UK would leave the single market and customs union, and trade with the EU under WTO rules. Upside? No expectations of free movement of people or the UK having to apply common EU tariffs on non-EU goods. Downsides? Tariffs and customs formalities would come into force on UK–EU trade, there'd be no preferential access to EU markets, and trade would be far from frictionless. It's worth noting that no major country trades with the EU solely on WTO terms.

What about trading with countries outside the EU after Brexit, after we're no longer covered by the EU's trade deals with those countries? For one thing, any new non-EU trade deals won't come into force until after the transition period has ended (we can negotiate and sign deals with countries during the transition period, but those deals won't apply until after the transition period).

REMEMBER

Critics of Brexit have noted that negotiating new trade deals with other countries may mean the UK is forced to accept goods that don't meet our current standards. Food safety and animal welfare are oft-quoted examples, particularly the famous "chlorine chicken." (The United States uses chemical washes, including chlorine, in some production processes — a practice that's banned in the EU.) Many UK consumers aren't exactly licking their lips at the thought of eating chlorinated chicken. And some UK businesses are understandably worried about competition from overseas producers that aren't subject to the same high standards as they are.

Meanwhile, many Brexit supporters point to the Commonwealth as a bright prospect in the UK's future trade relationships, which makes sense given the close bond the UK has with its Commonwealth partners. Yet, some of the same quality concerns may apply (for example, Australian beef is treated with hormones that are currently banned in the EU), and the EU is, for now, a much bigger export customer for UK businesses than the Commonwealth is.

All in all, expect trade negotiations to have more twists and turns than *Game of Thrones!* It'll certainly be interesting to see how all this plays out over the next few years.

The Irish Border

I've written already about the issues surrounding the potential "hard border" between Northern Ireland and the Republic of Ireland (see Chapter 3). I don't want to repeat what I said earlier, but it's worth mentioning the Irish border and backstop as a key issue to keep an eye on.

REMEMBER

Developments in this area will be especially relevant to companies in Northern Ireland and Ireland, because any hard border would impact integration and trade between the two countries. But even companies in England, Scotland, and Wales will need to stay informed, because goods moving between Northern Ireland and the rest of the UK may be subject to additional checks.

Scottish Independence

In 2014, Scotland held a referendum to decide whether Scotland should leave the UK and become an independent country. After what was a record turnout for a UK election, the result was a pretty confident "no," with 55.3 percent of voters opting to remain part of the UK.

Then the UK as a whole voted to leave the EU in 2016, even though Scottish voters were overwhelmingly in favor of staying in the EU.

In March 2017, Scottish First Minister Nicola Sturgeon formally announced she would seek approval for a second Scottish referendum. The Scottish government approved this request, but the UK government chose not to respond. In fact, at the time of writing, the UK government still hadn't formally responded. It's probably on someone's to-do list somewhere. . . .

REMEMBER

Those in favor of a second referendum argue that the UK leaving the EU constitutes a material change of circumstances. Those who are against a second referendum argue that Brexit is being used to push the agendas of pro-independence politicians.

Whether calls for a second referendum get louder or quietly disappear remains to be seen. But if there is a second referendum, and Scotland chooses independence, will Wales follow suit? And what will it mean for those in favor of unification between Ireland and Northern Ireland?

Repatriation of UK/EU Laws to Westminster and Devolved Parliaments

Assuming the UK exits the EU with a withdrawal agreement (see Chapter 3), the UK plans to keep EU laws during the transition period. Quite how much the UK will be able to change its laws after that isn't yet clear — much will depend on the international agreements we make with the EU and potentially other trade partners. Even if the UK ultimately decided to repeal and completely change all inherited EU laws (which is unlikely — just think of all the paperwork involved!), UK businesses wanting to trade in the EU would likely still have to comply broadly with certain EU laws.

But one thing is clear: having withdrawn from the EU, the UK (and not Brussels) will be responsible for setting its own laws. But where in the UK will those laws be made? After all, Scotland, Wales, and Northern Ireland have their own devolved parliaments.

REMEMBER

Devolution means that the UK's constituent countries have their own independent governments and parliaments. Each can set its own policies in certain areas, including health, education and agriculture. (Crucially, this doesn't apply to all policies, though. Things like benefits, immigration, and foreign policy remain under the overall control of Westminster. In other words, Wales can't take a different foreign policy stance than England.)

So, when the UK "takes back control of its laws," where does that control go to? In the first instance, all powers will come back to Westminster, and some will be devolved from there. But, to avoid disruption to the UK's own internal market, Westminster will want to see a UK-wide approach taken on certain areas (which may include devolved matters like agriculture and fishing).

In other words, whether Brexit leads to greater devolution of power (as some in the Scottish Vote Leave camp had speculated) or ends up restricting certain powers remains to be seen.

Will Companies Pull Out of the UK?

In February 2019, it was reported that the Netherlands was talking to 250 companies about switching their operations from the UK to the Netherlands, and the Dutch government boasted that it had already tempted more than 40 businesses or branch offices away from the UK.

High-profile companies that have already confirmed they're ditching the UK in favor of the Netherlands include Sony and Panasonic. But the Netherlands isn't the only European country trying to poach businesses. Other countries including Ireland, France, and Germany have also been trying to capitalize on Brexit and lure UK-based companies to their shores.

Whether your company is better off in Amsterdam or Aberdeen is something only you can answer. But assuming you're opting to stay put, be aware of trends within your industry pulling businesses out of the UK and into the EU. Their leaving could provide an opportunity to increase your market share and grab some of their customers (see Chapter 10).

The Changing Political Landscape in Britain

Many commentators felt that the popularity of the UK Independence Party (UKIP) wasn't just about a desire to pull out of the EU, but also a desire to give the middle finger to the mainstream establishment — a system that's seen British politics dominated (for the most part, at least) by two parties for centuries. The same could be said of Donald Trump being elected president in the United States — many voters responded positively to the fact that he wasn't a politician.

I'd love to say things have improved since the Brexit vote, that voters feel better having gotten their dislike of politicians off their chests. But that's not the sense I get. Thanks to all the political wrangling behind the withdrawal deal process (see Chapter 3), many in the UK find themselves rolling their eyes at shenanigans in Westminster. The inability of both main parties to find common ground and work together to create the best outcome disgusts many of the people I talk to. Plenty, on both sides of the Brexit debate, feel that politicians just aren't acting in the interests of the country.

Add to this the divisions within both the Labour and Conservative parties, and you have a whole lot of uncertainty and turmoil. So perhaps it was no surprise that, in February 2019, seven Labour Members of Parliament (MPs) quit the party to form their own breakaway, pro-EU Independent Group (later renamed Change UK), joined soon after by three Conservative MPs. And at the other end of the Brexit scale, Nigel Farage formed a new anti-EU party, the Brexit Party, in April 2019.

Will our wider political landscape change quite dramatically over the next few years? It'll be very interesting to see what happens at the next general election (scheduled for May 2022, but it could happen much sooner) — an election that may still be dominated by the Brexit fallout, whether we like it or not. And, of course, if the ruling party changes, that will mean a change in policies, which will further affect businesses. . . .

Workforce Pressures Affecting the Public and Private Sectors

Across the public and private sectors, there has been a lot of speculation about how Brexit will affect access to labor. Without wanting to repeat what I cover in Chapter 7 (which is all about employment and access to labor), this will be a key ongoing issue for many UK businesses.

The National Health Service (NHS) alone has around 63,000 employees from the EU, which accounts for 5 percent of the total NHS workforce. In the private sector, care homes and farming are also heavily reliant on overseas labor.

Circle back to Chapter 7 and use the checklists in Chapter 9 to assess potential staffing impacts on your business, and be sure to keep up to date on the latest immigration policy after Brexit.

Make sure your dream team of expert advisers (see Chapter 10) includes an employment law specialist who can help you understand implications and navigate policy changes.

The Impact on Currency and Financial Markets

We all know that worldwide currencies and stock markets are more volatile in times of political and economic uncertainty. The pound has certainly had a bouncy couple of years since the Brexit vote.

If your business is sensitive to currency exchange fluctuations (for example, if you import and export goods), talk to your accountant and financial adviser to see whether there are ways to limit your exposure.

But it's not just the value of the pound that fluctuates. Stock markets and property markets are typically volatile when there's political and economic uncertainty.

This volatility affects businesses in all sorts of ways, such as:

>> The value of businesses floated on the stock exchange tumbles.

>> Foreign investors are more likely to hold back investment.

>> Pension pots suffer.

REMEMBER

News outlets like the *Financial Times* are invaluable for business leaders at times like this, but you can also find useful insights on financial forums such as Citywire Funds Insider (http://moneyforums.citywire.co.uk) or Bull Market Board (www.bullmarketboard.com).

Accessing Helpful Resources to Help You Stay Up to Date

In addition to your regular news source, you may also want to regularly check the latest Brexit information from the following resources:

>> **Department for Exiting the European Union** (www.gov.uk/government/ organisations/department-for-exiting-the-european-union): Known by the snappy acronym DExEU, this is the government department responsible for overseeing Brexit negotiations.

>> **Confederation of British Industry** (www.cbi.org.uk/business-issues/ brexit-and-eu-negotiations): Representing 190,000 businesses across the UK, the CBI has a thorough handle on what Brexit means for companies.

>> **British Chambers of Commerce** (www.britishchambers.org.uk/page/ brexit): The BCC has lots of practical advice for companies and thoughtful analyses of Brexit developments.

>> **The Federation of Small Businesses** (www.fsb.org.uk/standing-up-for-you/brexit/introduction): FSB is a great resource for small businesses and people who are self-employed.

>> **Trade associations:** If your company is a member of a trade association, be sure to regularly check its latest Brexit guidance and advice.

Index

About the Author

Nicholas Wallwork is a leading international real estate market commentator, entrepreneur, businessman, investor, developer, and author. Nicholas heads up several real estate and investment companies and has produced and presented a number of real estate TV shows on Sky TV in the UK. As an author, he has written *Investing in International Real Estate For Dummies* (Wiley) and writes a multitude of educational content dedicated to supporting landlords, real estate professionals, and investors across the industry through www.propertyforum.com (a real estate chat forum, educational hub, and news portal) and www.bullmarketboard.com (a stock market investing chat forum, hub, and news portal). Nicholas and his team also run www.whitefinch.com, which is a specialist digital media marketing agency serving clients in the real estate, investment, and business worlds.

Through the Redbrick real estate brand, Nicholas, his business partners, and their team have a demonstrated track record of working on successful developments and investments in the real estate industry. Nicholas has a wide breadth of business, investment, and real estate experience with specific expertise in developing houses in multiple occupation, micro studio and co-living apartment blocks, and private rented-sector developments. He also has experience developing serviced apartments, healthcare properties, and assisted living properties.

Nicholas can be contacted at www.nicholaswallwork.com for any business enquiries. He is also on LinkedIn, Facebook, and Instagram (@nicholas_wallwork).

Dedication

This book is dedicated to my amazing wife and best friend, Britta Wallwork, and to my incredible, always positive family Siènna, Skyla, and Silàs. Britta you are always there for me and you're my soul mate. I couldn't have achieved half of what I have without your unwavering support through good times and well as tough times. Kids, I just hope to inspire you and leave you a lasting legacy to stay positive and remember to always keep dreaming big. You can do anything you decide to do!

Author's Acknowledgments

I never thought I'd be writing a book on Brexit so thank you to Katie Mohr and Tracy Boggier from Wiley for bringing me this unique opportunity! I'm very grateful and enjoyed rising to the challenge with my team to pull together all the research needed for this kind of book.

Tracy, thank you for your continued support and backing! It's an exciting journey we're on together, and I'm enjoying every minute. Lots of great opportunities keep arising, and I'm really looking forward to continuing to work with you on those and many more that are likely to come up!

A huge thank you to Elizabeth Kuball, my favorite project editor! Great to work with you again — it's always a pleasure!

I'd like to thank Veronika Yefremenko for working with me on the companion courses for *Investing in International Real Estate For Dummies* and getting that deal put together. Again, lots of opportunities we can build on there.

Thanks also go out to my wife and best friend, Britta Wallwork, and all my friends and family both here in the UK and also in Holland (where Britta is from!). Sorry, I can't name you all, but thanks for putting up with all my brainstorming and many harebrained ideas I've had over the years!

A huge thank-you to Chris Sturmer, my best friend and business partner. There's nothing better than working with someone you can absolutely trust in every sense of the word. We balance each other out, and the end result means we almost always make the right decisions. I'm truly grateful for everything, and I wouldn't want to go on this journey with anyone else.

A huge thank you to Claire for all your help, including organizing, research, planning, and support. I couldn't have done this without you. You're awesome and fantastic. Thank you! I look forward to working with you for many years to come.

Thanks so much to Mark Benson, who we work with closely in our various businesses. Mark your knowledge, research articles, and overall input have been invaluable to say the least. It's been a pleasure working with you for so long, and I hope we're working together for many more years to come!

Thanks to Robert and Paola! It's a pleasure working with you. Even though we've not been gifted anything easily, we're still building forward and I'm optimistic for the future.

Thanks also to some of my insanely talented, loyal, and supportive team: Kelly, Michelle, Stephanie, Kath, and Yan. We couldn't do it without you guys. A massive and heart felt *thank-you!*

Thank you to all our JV investors and lenders who have trusted and believed in us over the years. I'm proud we've been able to create win-win investments for us all.

Thank you to all my mentors, whether in person or "virtual mentors" (successful people I've followed over the years). I believe in continual learning from others, and I've built my whole wealth-building model around this philosophy.

Finally, thank you to all our clients, readers, and followers — I hope I can help by passing on some of this wisdom to you so you can create wealth, freedom, choice, success, and happiness for yourself.

Publisher's Acknowledgments

Associate Publisher: Katie Mohr

Project Editor: Elizabeth Kuball

Copy Editor: Elizabeth Kuball

Production Editor: Siddique Shaik

Cover Photo: © narvikk/Getty Images

Take dummies with you everywhere you go!

Whether you are excited about e-books, want more from the web, must have your mobile apps, or are swept up in social media, dummies makes everything easier.

Find us online!

dummies.com

Leverage the power

Dummies is the global leader in the reference category and one of the most trusted and highly regarded brands in the world. No longer just focused on books, customers now have access to the dummies content they need in the format they want. Together we'll craft a solution that engages your customers, stands out from the competition, and helps you meet your goals.

Advertising & Sponsorships

Connect with an engaged audience on a powerful multimedia site, and position your message alongside expert how-to content. Dummies.com is a one-stop shop for free, online information and know-how curated by a team of experts.

- Targeted ads
- Video
- Email Marketing

- Microsites
- Sweepstakes sponsorship

20 MILLION PAGE VIEWS EVERY SINGLE MONTH

15 MILLION UNIQUE VISITORS PER MONTH

43% OF ALL VISITORS ACCESS THE SITE VIA THEIR MOBILE DEVICES

700,000 NEWSLETTER SUBSCRIPTIONS TO THE INBOXES OF

300,000 UNIQUE INDIVIDUALS EVERY WEEK

# of dummies

Custom Publishing

Reach a global audience in any language by creating a solution that will differentiate you from competitors, amplify your message, and encourage customers to make a buying decision.

- Apps
- Books
- eBooks
- Video
- Audio
- Webinars

Brand Licensing & Content

Leverage the strength of the world's most popular reference brand to reach new audiences and channels of distribution.

For more information, visit dummies.com/biz

PERSONAL ENRICHMENT

Staying Sharp	Facebook	Guitar	Investing	Beekeeping	Digital Photography
9781119187790	9781119179030	9781119293354	9781119293347	9781119310068	9781119235606
USA $26.00	USA $21.99	USA $24.99	USA $22.99	USA $22.99	USA $24.99
CAN $31.99	CAN $25.99	CAN $29.99	CAN $27.99	CAN $27.99	CAN $29.99
UK £19.99	UK £16.99	UK £17.99	UK £16.99	UK £16.99	UK £17.99

Meditation	Pregnancy	Samsung Galaxy S7	iPhone	Crocheting	Nutrition
9781119251163	9781119235491	9781119279952	9781119283133	9781119287117	9781119130246
USA $24.99	USA $26.99	USA $24.99	USA $24.99	USA $24.99	USA $22.99
CAN $29.99	CAN $31.99	CAN $29.99	CAN $29.99	CAN $29.99	CAN $27.99
UK £17.99	UK £19.99	UK £17.99	UK £17.99	UK £16.99	UK £16.99

PROFESSIONAL DEVELOPMENT

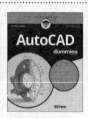

Windows 10	AutoCAD	Excel 2016	QuickBooks 2017	macOS Sierra	LinkedIn	Windows 10
9781119311041	9781119255796	9781119293439	9781119281467	9781119280651	9781119251132	9781119310563
USA $24.99	USA $39.99	USA $26.99	USA $26.99	USA $29.99	USA $24.99	USA $34.00
CAN $29.99	CAN $47.99	CAN $31.99	CAN $31.99	CAN $35.99	CAN $29.99	CAN $41.99
UK £17.99	UK £27.99	UK £19.99	UK £19.99	UK £21.99	UK £17.99	UK £24.99

SharePoint 2016	Fundamental Analysis	Networking	Office 2016	Office 365	Salesforce.com	Coding
9781119181705	9781119263593	9781119257769	9781119293477	9781119265313	9781119239314	9781119293323
USA $29.99	USA $26.99	USA $29.99	USA $26.99	USA $24.99	USA $29.99	USA $29.99
CAN $35.99	CAN $31.99	CAN $35.99	CAN $31.99	CAN $29.99	CAN $35.99	CAN $35.99
UK £21.99	UK £19.99	UK £21.99	UK £19.99	UK £17.99	UK £21.99	UK £21.99

dummies.com

dummies®
A Wiley Brand

Learning Made Easy

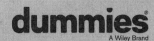

Small books for big imaginations

9781119177173
USA $9.99
CAN $9.99
UK £8.99

9781119177272
USA $9.99
CAN $9.99
UK £8.99

9781119177241
USA $9.99
CAN $9.99
UK £8.99

9781119177210
USA $9.99
CAN $9.99
UK £8.99

9781119262657
USA $9.99
CAN $9.99
UK £6.99

9781119291336
USA $9.99
CAN $9.99
UK £6.99

9781119233527
USA $9.99
CAN $9.99
UK £6.99

9781119291220
USA $9.99
CAN $9.99
UK £6.99

9781119177302
USA $9.99
CAN $9.99
UK £8.99

Unleash Their Creativity

dummies.com

dummies
A Wiley Brand